Working-Class Queers

'A much needed and timely deep forensic dive into the underrepresentation of working-class queers within our queer structures and concepts.'

—Juno Roche, writer

'This work holds rich and deep insights into lived experience, the power lines of learning within institutions, how people act on and transform each other in community. Yvette's book opens doors and transforms fault lines. It will be beneficial to thinkers, feelers and doers for years to come.'

—Sarah Schulman, author of *Let the Record Show: A Political History of ACT UP New York*

'Building on more than two decades of engaged research with LGBT+ communities, *Working-Class Queers* makes a major contribution to queer feminist methods. A must-read for thinkers asking about the how of queer and lesbian studies in troubled and hopeful times alike.'

—Matt Brim, Professor of Queer Studies at the College of Staten Island, City University of New York.

Working-Class Queers
Time, Place and Politics

Yvette Taylor

PLUTO  PRESS

First published 2023 by Pluto Press
New Wing, Somerset House, Strand, London WC2R 1LA
and Pluto Press, Inc.
1930 Village Center Circle, 3-834, Las Vegas, NV 89134

www.plutobooks.com

British Library Cataloguing in Publication Data
A catalogue record for this book is available from the British Library

ISBN   978 0 7453 4102 6   Paperback
ISBN   978 1 78680 807 3   PDF
ISBN   978 1 78680 808 0   EPUB

Typeset by Stanford DTP Services, Northampton, England

Simultaneously printed in the United Kingdom and United States of America

Contents

List of Figures   vii
Acknowledgements   viii

1. Fighting for the Queer Left   1
The outness of queer: researching class and sexuality
over the long-term   10
The queer case: categories and cases   17

2. (Un)Doing Queer-Class Data   20
Being data: 'where are you from?'   22
Doing data: queer/class   34

3. Queer Life in the Pandemic   42
Key-Queer workers?   44
Chronic conditions   49
Reasonable adjustments: mutual aid and non-state support   55
Conclusions: breaking the circuit   60

4. Queer Provincialisms in (Post-)Brexit Britain   62
Project-ing whiteness: working with (white) Europe   64
World citizens in 'Rainbow Europe'   70
Queer in a wee place: from Little Britain to Big Scotland?   77
Conclusion: queer possibilities in thinking beyond the state   81

5. Queers and Austerity   83
Academia, outreach, and austerity or becoming
middle-class?   86
Austerity scenes   89
Conclusion: beyond an austerity of imagination   106

6. Queer Anachronisms: Working-Class Lesbians Out of Time and Place   108
Lesbians of colour, trans lesbians, queer lesbians   116
Conclusion: political cares   127

7. Towards a Queer Working-Class Reading List   128
The feminist classroom: from the bottom reading group
to a room of her own?   134
Queer classrooms   143

Appendix: Texts Referred to in the Auto-Reply Reading List   156   160

Notes   163
Index   187

List of figures

0.1   'Working-Class Queers' Call for Participants Poster   x

2.1 and 2.2   Images from 'Making Space for Queer-Identifying
Religious Youth' research: 'You have taken away my identity'
and 'Queer Identity and Religion' map   23

2.3   Location of Glasgow Women's Library, 1994–2007   33

2.4   Glasgow Women's Library Queer/Class workshop, 2020,
'In the hands of the proletariat'   36

2.5   Glasgow Women's Library Archive, photographed 2019   37

2.6   Glasgow Women's Library Queer/Class workshop, 2020,
Inscription on table   39

2.7   Glasgow Women's Library Queer/Class workshop,
2020, 'Equal opportunities' box   40

3.1   Postcard image completed by interviewees, 2020–22   42

7.1   'Outwrite Women's Newspaper', Glasgow Women's
Library   129

7.2   Official Picket poster, 2018   130

7.3   Reading-writing list, 2021–22   131

7.4   Creating Feminist Classrooms feedback prompt,
2001–21   152

7.5 and 7.6   Who's Here? Who's Queer? workshop, 2022:
'My queer box' and 'Resources'   154

7.7 and 7.8   From 'Early Career Researchers' workshop,
2012: 'Back to Square 1?' and 'The PhD wall'   155

7.9   Queer bookends, 2022   158

Acknowledgements

This book was written during a global pandemic, during austerity, during global recession, and into the cost-of-living crisis. To write this is to acknowledge the times we're in, as stretching backwards and forwards. To write now is to complicate crisis as exceptional, resolved by DIY individualism, resource management, austerity, deferral … or in keeping writing. And yet I have kept writing, enabled and supported by people in and beyond these book pages and often as queer-feminist solidarity and persistence. I write, hopeful of something different rather than a return to 'business as usual'. In this book I ask if this might be a queer-left hope, animated by working-class queer life.

To rewrite our projects, embodied as parts of ourselves, means revisiting data – going back through official and unofficial archives, records, readings, places, and feelings. Such data is represented between these pages, structured into chapters, headings, and sub-headings and made neat, even as it surpasses the pages. Queer data in particular might be thought of as excessive, weighty, emotional: the data in-between and beyond these pages weighs down on me and rightly does so as a demand for attention. But it also weighs as practice, as a continual redoing, rewriting, and rethinking about how and why class and sexuality come to matter.

Thanks to everyone who has shared ideas and encouragement as Working-Class Queers took shape: thanks to Matt Brim, Samuele Grassi, Emily Henderson, Mariya Ivancheva, Ben Rogaly, Heather Shipley, Jane Traies, Jacqueline Ullman, Alice Walker, Claire Wilson, and Sarah Wilson. I thank everyone who has been part of my academic past and present, and special thanks to Michelle Addison, Maddie Breeze, and Cristina Costa for making the journeys worthwhile. Thanks to colleagues in the School of Education and in the wider School of Humanities and Social Sciences at the University of Strathclyde, including members of the Strathclyde University Feminist Research Network.

Special thanks to those who have collaborated and been employed on some of the projects drawn upon in this book. In the 'Bright Lights, Big City' project, this included Michelle Addison, Mark Casey, and Megan Todd. Karen Cuthbert, Emily Falconer and Ria Snowdon were researchers on the 'Making Space for Queer Identifying Religious Youth' project. Maja B. Andreasen, Claire Goodfellow, and Matson Lawrence were researchers on the 'Comparing Intersectional Life Course Inequalities amongst LGBTQI+ Citizens in Four European Countries' (CILIA) project: thanks to CILIA colleagues in Berlin (Yener Bayramoglu, María do Mar Castro Varela), England (Sait Bayrakdar, Andrew King), and Portugal (Rita Alcaire, Ana Cristina Santos, Ana Lucia Santos). Sincere thanks to collaborative external partners, and funding bodies (the Economic and Social Research Council and the British Academy). Thanks to Samia Singh for all ongoing creative inputs and collaborations. In 2020–21 I undertook a fellowship at the Scottish Parliament and I'm grateful for the support and advice from Nicki Georghiou and Simon Wakefield.

The data in this book draws upon research carried out across two decades, involving interviews with more than 250 people: I am truly grateful to all participants. Thanks to Neda Tehrani at Pluto for all the understanding and encouragement through difficult times. This book wouldn't have been possible without the love, generosity, humour and support of Churnjeet Mahn: thank you.

Figure 0.1 'Working-Class Queers' Call for Participants Poster.
Source: Samia Singh.

1

Fighting for the Queer Left

'A Bed of Roses'
I am writing to express the distress and anger I feel about the bigoted intolerance towards white, educated, 'middle-class' women ... on what basis do the self-styled working-class want to categorise other women, and in doing so promote disharmony amongst us? Father's occupation? Husband's? Own (if employed)? ... On the one hand they call for equal access to education and higher-level jobs, then sneer at 'middle-class educational values' and reject those of us who have benefitted by such access, calling us 'over-educated' and 'over-privileged'. If we currently enjoy those things which they say all women <u>should</u> have, if we offer to share the particular skills we have acquired – e.g. how to use the system – we are accused of being patronizing 'do-gooders', but if we don't, then we are colluding with the patriarchal system in their oppression ... In any case, being 'middle-class' doesn't automatically mean that life is a bed of roses.
　　　　—Glasgow Women's Library, Lesbian Archive, Box File 1

'I'm a Working-class Woman O.K.'
I went along to this workshop feeling quite excited, proudly wearing my badge saying 'I'm a Working-class Woman O.K.', but came away completely disillusioned by the aggression that had been displayed and feeling that I had been indirectly attacked for being a lesbian ... for doing consciousness-raising (a middle-class indulgence), for wearing dungarees (uniform of the middle-class) ... Anyone who was in any way articulate or spoke with a middle-class accent was usually cut short or constantly interrupted. When those with a notably working-class accent spoke, there was complete silence and even applause at the end.[1]
　　　　—Glasgow Women's Library, Lesbian Archive, Box File 2

1

Working-Class Queers draws on data from 2001 to 2021,[2] as a long-term project persistently returning to questions of sexuality and class. As a culmination of more than two decades of UK-based research, it has a past that precedes it, a present that it persists through, and a future that it hopes for. It overlaps – and is sometimes at odds – with my own professional and personal life. Sometimes going forward means going backwards. Sometimes we go back through archives as embodied journeys (un)doing our own data, and as reluctant returns, frustrations, and repetitions: 'I'm a Working-class Woman O.K.' becomes a queer claim in this non-linear forward–backward movement between data gathering, doing data, and being data.

As an undergraduate, I attended university in a different socio-political climate, benefiting from a full maintenance grant as a student from a working-class background. I live with the sense of getting into higher education just in time, before escalating costs from the New Labour period onwards, notably through the notorious Conservative–Liberal Democrats (2010–15) coalition government pact of increased tuition fees, positioned as a debt-absorbing investment in oneself. I imagined a different future in going to university – and still believe universities can offer access to and realisation of different futures. But my sense of optimism isn't wholly tied to individual financial return. Queer-feminist educators have always insisted on learning as socially transformative, as a commitment to social futures, rather than as a static essence, or as an investment in individual future selves (ourselves).

As a student in the '90s I attended a three-day long Marxism Now conference in London, with regional representation from across the UK: I opted into the Glasgow bus trip to London and benefited from the free place and free lunch. I experienced London cosmopolitanism, going into LGBTQ+ venues with some trepidation, before returning to the conference space and hearing some of the Left's political greats, such as Tony Benn. I remember other, maybe queerer, spaces, in classrooms and corridors on the edge of campus, and I remember giggling at the (over)use of 'comrades', as participants politicised identifications, in some of the same and different ways conveyed in frustrated badge-wearing at feminist conferences (see the opening extracts in this chapter). In many ways, the move in and out of conference space (held in prestigious university premises) and scene space (lacking prestige, investment, or capital) represented the cross-over and disjuncture between queer-left agendas. As a young queer working-class person, I optimistically hoped for a future, which over the past two decades has been increasingly at odds with and disconnected from mainstream political shifts and, often, from queer or left politics.

Looking back and forward, through events, data, and career changes, embodied in the queer-feminist researcher (me) causes pause, disappointment, and hope. Across reading, researching, teaching, and writing efforts, I've experienced career mobility, even if queerly so – I've crossed disciplines, moved cities, and researched and taught at different 'types' of UK universities.[3] Without really knowing it, I started this project as part of a circular route away from and back to Scotland, having lived and worked in various parts of England – York, Newcastle, and London – since 2000. Moving institutions and departing 'cosmopolitan' London, I retraced my steps north. Having lived and worked in the 'provincial' North East of England for ten years, I relocated back to Scotland at the end of 2015. In many ways Glasgow, and Scotland, were changed places. Devolution and independence efforts arguably allow constituent UK nations to claim different futures – as still part of a collective European politics, as more socially democratic and left-of-centre, or as better at managing health crises or persisting socio-economic divisions. Much can be claimed through imagining difference or exceptionalism as a turning point: national progression and distinction is announced and celebrated in the headlines of the UK's LGBT Action Plan (2018), also evident in the Scottish Parliament's announcement of being 'world-leading' with their LGBT Inclusive Curriculum.[4]

This period saw increased claims around a supposed Scottish *difference*, through politics, culture, or even character.[5] In the aftermath of the Scottish independence referendum (2014) and the run-up to the European Union referendum (2016), and subsequent transition period leading to Brexit (2020), places of difference have mattered (and Scotland now makes rather bold claims about its 'world-leading' difference). But the council estate I grew up in *still* rates similarly, and badly, now as then, in terms of poor health, housing, employment prospects, and life expectancy. The Scotland I remembered, and realised again on return, was often still a place of sexism, racism, homophobia, and transphobia, and of escalating poverty and inequality. Some endurances are embodied, while not always static: my accent changes over again, known and placed in Scotland, un-placed in England, where it's encompassed as just Scottish. How this is felt, as relief or otherwise, anonymity or identity, movement or lack of, maps onto class and sexuality, as politicised, professional, and personal inhabitations. I can say I'm the first person in my family to go to university, and I can say that I am a university professor, a lesbian, a feminist, a queer. What happens when these backgrounds are put to work in foregrounding queer intersectional thinking, re-activating the queer left?

Over two decades I've moved from being a student to being a teacher. I work in the politicised context of ongoing University and College Union (UCU) strike action. Higher education has not been immune to financialisation, or crises, as widening participation is constituted as a new marketing opportunity, a reaching out to new 'diversities', whether imagined as working-class students, international students, or LGBTQ+ students.[6] In reflecting back and forward in and through education, I ask if 'the queer' and 'the left' are aiming for the same future, and if a queer left might be possible. How will class knowledge, methods, and theorisation take account of queer – will they only nod at intersectionality as a catch-all gesture towards the queer-to-be-included? What can we learn by using class as a lens to understand queer sexuality in the context of the nation state over the past two decades? If life really has 'got better' for queers in the UK, what kinds of queers have been rewarded as good citizens? Who has been left behind? What happens when we lose class critique in queer politics and social analysis? In thinking about (inter)disciplinary research productions, I am still compelled by class as a concept, and one which still often collides with queer. In this book I consider queer *and* class, including dimensions of the political, affective, archival, material, and personal:

You can always tell a real working-class person because they want to be middle-class. Not the culture of middle-class but they want

4

a good salary, and they want the money, and they don't disdain those things. I've got colleagues who'll be like 'everybody should get paid the same', and I used to say all of that stuff as well. But it is, it'll be working-class job applicants at a senior level who'll be like 'no you fucking pay me my salary!', do you know what I mean? 'I crawled over cut glass to get here. Pay me my salary'. It's only middle-class people that romanticise being poor ... I mean I'm still absolutely really wildly disordered about money because of being under-resourced and neglected in childhood. Like I have, if my bank card goes out of date and it beeps and doesn't run I have a full-blown panic attack, and I'm forty-eight years old and I know there's money in my bank account.

—Senior manager in UK LGBTQ+ organisation,
interviewed 2021

In interviewees' efforts and insistences ('I crawled over cut glass to get here. Pay me my salary'), I recognise class. I choose to repeat class queerly and across time and place – from the workshop to the archive, from the classroom to the fieldwork site – noting its elisions and erasures, as well as contemporary classifications and re-circulations. The opening letter extracts are from the Lesbian Archives at Glasgow Women's Library (GWL). Old concepts, words and thoughts reside there, but they also endure and animate the present. The first extract highlights women's misfit with traditional heteronormative class analysis, classificatory struggles around 'pigeonholing', and possible normative and anti-normative actions. Privilege becomes wrapped in scare quotes, alongside 'over-educated' and 'middle-class'. In claiming that 'I'm a Working-Class Woman O.K.', the second extract bemoans the 'constant interruption' that follows, even in an affirming, applauding space – class reversals, sneering snobbery, implied shame, and explicit aggression all feature. These words constitute interruptions and repetitions, as class interrupts feminist space, as queer interrupts recognisable classed signs and associations, and as white, middle-classness is repeated as the entitled but aggrieved wounded subject.

Sat in the archives at GWL I searched a range of local and national feminist publications, dwelling on the emotional and material wounds of persisting patriarchy, capitalism, and heterosexism across the years, as enduring structures despite liberal policy shifts. In countless newsletters there are features, full-page articles, and multiple letters of classed interruptions to what feminism and feminists are, to what and who lesbians are, and to whether queer might stretch or solidify these terms. In many ways the classed conversations of 'then', the 1970s, '80s, and '90s, are repeated in the 'now', with the archival box files placed next to me forming a high and weighty pile of evidence across time. My fingers became dusty, and my eyes strained, as I dwelt on and in these living histories. These were and are lively archives, resonating across time and place, pulling us back and propelling us forward: I laughed in reading the full back-and-forward 'bust up' that the opening letter extracts convey. My laughter echoed in the now regenerated and relocated prize-winning library that I once inhabited in my teens and twenties in the late 1990s and early 2000s, then located in a smelly dimly lit backstreet lane. My partner and I now joke that we might well have been sitting back-to-back in the cold damp building, having braved the broken lift, as we read 'lesbian facts' and allowed ourselves to imagine what LGBTQ+ life might be like... Had queer been constructed for, or within reach of, working-class queers, or has it, us, them, been deconstructed and decomposed, along with the old decaying GWL building?

The 'bust ups' in and beyond pages, whether community or academic, are still known and felt across the LGBTQ+ community. Life is still not 'a bed of roses' for many queers, despite a slew of legislation and, often uneasy, incorporation – into workplaces as 'diversity', into the calendar year as #LGBTHistoryMonth, into schools as rainbow-coloured curriculum cladding. Being at GWL, and reading a distinctly Scottish queer archive, off-centre from global (US) mappings of Queer Theory, means being firmly located, where questions of location, reflexivity and standpoint are never far from the feminist map. My partner and I are both Scottish and from Glasgow; I'm white and she is South Asian. We've departed and returned, and Glasgow maps us whether we like it or not. I'm often recognised as being from Glasgow (and from a particular part of Glasgow), while often she is not: this (mis)recognition is repeated, again and again, including at a recent queering-the-map event where people were invited to co-produce Glasgow's queer past, present, and future.

Glasgow represents itself as an authentically working-class, down-to-earth, unpretentious city. But not everyone is included or recognised in this claim, which is also a gendered and racialised one, figured through masculinity and whiteness. My partner grew up bilingual and is often told she doesn't have a Glaswegian accent. She's told she grew up in the posh 'West End', which wasn't the posh West End when she was growing up, but a space of white-flight, as white working-class people left in an attempt to retain value in moving away from their South Asian neighbours. The white middle-classes have now moved in, and in doing so have extended themselves and the boundary of what constitutes the 'West End', and 'West-Enders'. They celebrate 'multiculturalism', pulling her in while pushing her out, not cognisant of the work of code-switching[7] involved in alternating between two languages. My partner is often not recognised as bilingual, an association seemingly more easily attributable to modern language speakers; incorrectly, she was placed into the English-as-a-second-language group at school, as I differently sat in the 'bottom reading' group. We think about possibly sitting back-to-back in classroom settings and recognise the class-race sorting and subverting that continues to entangle categories, experiences and emotions across time and place.

We hold our irritation between us, deflecting misrecognition. We attend a feminist event and she's asked if she's 'out' to her family: family seems to follow her, while I'm rarely asked about mine, assumed to be 'ambitious', so unattached and without the 'weight' of family that 'career success' would, and does, disallow for women. Ambition is gendered, classed, and racialised, and white middle-class women are often the beneficiaries of 'equality, diversity, and inclusion' initiatives.[8] Closet doors are summoned, prised open and peered into by a well-meaning white, middle-class, young, out, queer, just as they are during the annual LGBT History Month, Black History Month, International Women's Day, and so on. The well-meaning one continues as we stall, telling us that 'lesbian' is a less expansive term, that queer does and says more. I feel this as an interruption and a repetition – to the term 'lesbian', to the story of 'outness', to the (im)possibility of being and doing

7

'queer' – and to the precarity of our positions when (de)legitima-
tised through race and class. Feminism – and the lesbian feminist
in particular – risks being read as the stall, as a TERF, a trans-exclusionary radical feminist. Knowing and feeling this makes me pause
on the political potential of a queer corrective here. In this book
I open up empirical enquiry to shifting and contested identifications, while refusing 'lesbian' as a singular, straight, or right-wing
signifier, politically appropriated: this is not the past, present, or
future that I recognise or hope for.

Such correctives become the 'common ground' that interviewees
have shared across time and place. This has included express-
ing class solidarities, which are then shattered by experiences of
racism, or rendered seemingly impossible when middle-class
queer parents buy-in to middle-class privilege, acting in the 'best
interests' of their children (an interest historically denied and even
criminalised). Common ground has stretched across expressions
of disbelief ('Is this useful?') that I am interested in working-class
queer lives, to having to pull out and pay attention when interviewees state things simply as obvious truths ('It's just like trans and
race is like bread and butter to me'—Nneka, 23, mixed race, pansexual lesbian, trans woman, interviewed 2019). My investment in
working-class queers is an embodied, political and material investment in the data, literature, objects, boxes, carried across time
and place as I've moved across disciplines, institutions, and UK
cities. My box file contains many articles criticising the focus on
white, Western, urban, middle-class gay male subjects. Contents
connect political economy and culture, including in the formation and incorporation of LGBTQ+ communities,[9] and via city
regenerations of commercialised scene spaces.[10] Contents exceed
the inclusion of same-sex rights, such as marriage,[11] into a box
which fits, highlighting the limits of liberal inclusion, disrupted by
queer-class commonalities.[12] But such common ground becomes
weighted as evidence of potential lag and lack.

The (post-)Brexit UK climate sees a repetition of working-
classness as deficit, as outside of Rainbow Europe pink-washing
('People think working-class council estates are Brexit crazy
unionists, racist, homophobic, there's no place for us there, there's
no LGBTQ there. Which is just a lie, which is just not true'—Dan,

36, white, gay cis man, interviewed 2020). But working-class queers never fitted into (other, continued) crisis times, still living with and through austerity periods, pandemic and cost-of-living-crisis times. As a feminist project that has persisted, this book tracks what follows across the fieldwork period (2001–21) and in 'crisis times': what can be learnt in researching class and sexuality over the long-term, as continued crises are remade via heightened inequalities, austerity regimes, welfare demolition, and the local–global re-bordering in neoliberal Britain? The decline of left politics, the promise and failure of a 'third way', the dismantling of the welfare state, and the escalation of right-wing populism as mainstream political presences, even with uneasy 'feminist' alliances, seem to represent the times we're in. Such times constitute a persisting 'hostile environment', where the crises of austerity, Brexit, and the COVID-19 pandemic follow on from and compound one another. The experiences of working-class queers offer an empirical refocus on the push-and-pull of normative successes, and the lack of fit as responsible citizens, privatised families, happy workers, or competitive consumers. Working-class queers often pragmatically persist through these mis-fits nonetheless, living with failure and re-engaging in a 'disappointing world'.[13]

Using 'class' as a term, concept, or identity can risk reserving it for or authenticating it as the supposedly real (white, straight, male) working-class, thereby playing into the hands of conservative agendas by displacing a sense of globalised working-classness across nation states, while also sidelining intersecting inequalities.[14] Such tensions exist within a broader political economy, which includes the demise of the political left, both nationally and globally. In the UK context, the past two decades have been shaped by those preceding them: notably, the Thatcher era; the rise of centrist New Labour; the heightening of neoliberalism; the retraction of the welfare state; the increased financialisation of key institutions and public life and the reign of the free market as solutions to crisis – witnessed most recently in Brexit and in contemporary post-pandemic times.

I use the section below, 'The Outness of Queer: Researching Class and Sexuality over the Long-Term', to outline the research projects that this book draws upon, as well as the book's structure: I'll chart my own research positionality and queer-class methods in Chapter 2. This leads to the empirical queer-class projects at the heart of this book (Chapters 3–6). As part of re-locating and re-engaging the possibilities and persistence of feminism, I explore the shifting landscape of feminist, queer, and class scholarship in Chapter 7. I think through the situatedness of academic productions as always occurring in time and place, when new terms and articulations may repeat or disguise; for example, 'precarity' as a term of now may act to displace 'class' as a term of then (or 'them'). I end by moving back to, and forwards through, a queer working-class reading list.

THE OUTNESS OF QUEER: RESEARCHING CLASS AND SEXUALITY OVER THE LONG-TERM

She had quite a strong working-class identity, she grew up around the miners' strike, so it's a very *different* kind of work-ing-class experience, but when I used to say things she'd say 'Yeah!' It kinda astounded me, it was the first time I thought 'This isn't just to do with being Asian', and being brought up in this Asian environment when my parents didn't work, it's also about something bigger than that ...
—Asifa, 29, South Asian, lesbian, interviewed 2002, England

I imagine my future at all points as being someone who is not fitting in, and I think sometimes structurally that means that the world is not for you.
—Alisha, 39, South Asian, lesbian, interviewed 2020, Scotland

There are similarities and differences within and between Alisha's and Asifa's accounts, and when figured alongside structuring contexts of gender, race and class, supposedly new conditions may be viewed as enduring realities, as still (not) fitting in. Questions of class – a term with an expansive socio-political and interdisci-plinary history – have *also and always* exceeded a numerical count, expressed as embodied states, privileges, and precarious claims. Debates have shifted class from an undead 'zombie category' to a conveyer of social, cultural, and economic worth, from being a descriptive 'socio-economic classification' to a survey 'experiment', and from a source of politicised identification to one of dis-identification. Recent contributions are valuable in rethinking, updating, and interrupting go-to terms, including as personal, professional, and politicised expressions.[15] We always need to be attentive to the work our terms do, and who is pulled along or left behind.

In interviewing working-class queers over a number of decades, I've witnessed what 'queer materiality' means up close and personal, even if buffered by queer networks, scene spaces, and families of choice. My research participants have faced homelessness, poor housing, unemployment, underemployment, educational exclusion, workplace discrimination, precarity, benefits cuts, inadequate health services, and racism, sexism, homophobia, and transphobia. In focus groups, interviews, workshops, in other people's homes and in mine, in fought-for and fraught-through LGBTQ+ community space, and in spaces such as churches, parks, food banks, schools, and playgrounds, I've researched different queer-class lives in the UK. I've done 'public sociology', as energising and exhausting: I've been involved in the pursuit of healthcare, housing, and benefits entitlement for interviewees – pursuits not conveyed in the ethics pages of university research committees, or easily captured as academic use or impact. These experiences are more than an appendix to proper theory or policy progression, and they also surpass a listing of individual associations or characteristics ('hard-working', 'undeserving', 'failing', 'ambitious'), instead being understood as social and collective.

Asifa's account, situated in the early 2000s, is one of finding other working-class queers, including in Manchester's commercially regenerated *Queer as Folk*[16] scene space. I remember meeting Asifa in a queer community centre and later going out on Canal Street, full of youthful optimism – in my twenties – thrilled by the only women's bar. Differently, the seemingly old, dated politics – of working-class communities and trade unionism – provided Asifa with a sense of 'something bigger', across racial–sexual difference. As an intimate connection linking into collective consciousness, Asifa's account rings true. But it is a truth disappeared in the reductive recasting of working-class life as male, white, and heterosexual. New Labour ideas on multicultural citizenship were soon ditched when minority ethnic groups, and Muslims in particular, were instructed to integrate into British society in the wake of 9/11 and the 7/7 London bombings.[17] Policies protecting and penalising those imagined as (to-be) included citizens and those pushed out as not-yet (not ever) British, actively mobilise gender and sexuality, witnessed then and now in the call against the 'war on terrorism', with LGBTQ+ groups seen as in need of protection from religious and racialised others.[18]

In the early 2000s, the New Labour (1997–2010) government was in its first term. It had already made bold claims on class and on gender, with 'Blair's Babes' becoming a sign that gender, like class, was over ('The class war is over. But the struggle for true equality has only just begun'[19]). Many have traced the political shifts during this time, when we were told things could only get better, a line used by New Labour in the 1997 election campaign. Election victory held the promise of a reversal of the socio-economic transformation of Britain, impacted by nearly 18 years of Conservative government, minus the inclusion of left-wing ideas ('We have rejected the worst of our past and rediscovered the best'). The electorate were positioned as individuals, rather than groups, communities, or collectives (such as unions), to be capacitated via education, employment and family. In these re-orderings, from structurally significant categories and collectivities to individuals and families, LGBTQ+ people were increasingly positioned as part of the right kind of diversity, assuming white, middle-class visibility. In standardising the age of consent, ending the ban of LGBT people from the armed forces, extending adoption rights, and creating civil partnerships, New Labour could be viewed as proactive in driving forward 'sexual citizenship', for some.

Within this context I started the fieldwork for what became *Working-Class Lesbian Life: Classed Outsiders* (2007), which included over 50 interviews and focus groups across England and Scotland. This study took place around the repeal of the UK's Section 28, legislation that had been introduced in 1988 by the Conservative government which banned local authorities from promoting homosexuality as a *pretended* family unit. In Scotland, I was part of anti-homophobic activism and protests – or 'real politics' – mobilised against the conservative Keep the Clause campaign and funded by millionaire businessman Brian Souter.[20]

This was a time of almost daily homophobia, but it was also a time of queer resistance, of incorporation and mainstreaming, with LGBTQ+ businesses and institutions impacting on 'Gay as Now' urban regeneration via commercialised scene spaces as leisure sites and touristic destinations – including for straight consumers. UK Legislation enacted between 2000 to 2003 banned Section 28, hailed as a success of New Labour (prompted initially by the newly formed Scottish Executive). But the queer left had not arrived, and the promise of things getting better was already wearing thin, becoming stretched and exhausted.

From the late 2000s, as the financial crisis hit and New Labour's 'third way' was thoroughly undermined, the Conservative–Liberal coalition government came to power, ramping up tuition fees in England and Wales, with the Liberal Democrats going back on their pre-election promises. I started researching educational exclusions, specifically those navigated by lesbian and gay parents in exercising their new citizenship entitlements as legitimate families. This project became *Lesbian and Gay Parenting: Securing Social and Educational Capitals* (2009).[21] As some parents were confidently capitalising on their status, others were once again experiencing the retraction of the welfare state, via benefits cuts, stigmatisation, and a shutting down of community, educational, and social resources. While the Conservatives framed austerity as a response to the 2008 financial crisis, the 'politics of austerity' refers both to austerity policies themselves and to the political discourses and cultural mechanisms, including stigma, used to justify and legitimate them. Welfare policies implemented by the coalition and Conservative governments since 2010 included the various changes introduced in the Welfare Reform Act 2012. Claimants of Personal Independence Payment (PIP), which replaced Disability Living Allowance (DLA), needed to undergo a Work Capability Assessment (WCA) to prove their eligibility.[22] I became intimately familiar with these assessments, the consequences of which are still playing out.

Sharply aware of the pressures of family, and the way it was overloaded with promise, I turned to parenting as a contested site for queers, in-between supposedly progressive and extremely regressive policy moments. Just as queers had been 'selling out' to mainstream market forces, the respectable lesbian and gay domestic couple became 'homonormative' in their state-sanctioned lifestyles.[23] Where queer families had long been accused of jeopardising the best interests of children, hearing lesbian and gay parents say they could indeed resource 'best interests' represented an interesting moment – a sign of political entitlement, perhaps, but one which often ended up situating 'poor parenting' and wrong 'choices' (educational, residential) back with more working-class parents. This happened amidst the closure of UK Sure Start programmes and a range of child-care and family welfare services which had aimed to give children the best start in life through state resources: in pulling such supports these futures were effectively privatised, financialised, and returned to The Family. Yet many middle-class participants in the 'Lesbian and Gay Parenting' project spoke of being *different* and selective choosers – from routes into parenting to accessing the best rainbow playgroup – rather than being the *same* as heterosexual parents. Queer discernment and capital were part of managing and making the 'good mix'. Class and race were mobilised as resources, as acquisitive exposure to the 'other', which they and their children could learn (and/or distance) from: lesbian and gay parenting could be understood as a project of whiteness, as much as a project of class.[24]

Religion, like family, is a state-sanctioned institution, and one which is differently lived in, and subject to misrepresentation and politicisation. Contestations within the category of queer – being too queer, or not queer enough – were central to the 'Making Space for Queer Identifying Religious Youth' project. The project commenced not long after the Equality Act 2010 established a set of 'protected characteristics', pitting some 'equalities' as contradicting or cancelling others. The UK and other Western nation states re-imagined themselves as protectors and liberators of (white, secular/Christian) LGBT citizens, awkwardly mobilising sexuality, race and religion.[25] In exploring religion, I was writing against the prevailing trend, which places it in contradiction to sexuality, as inevitably clashing sites or competing 'protected characteristics', a collision which becomes racialised and racist, as whiteness and Christianity remain unnamed backdrops to racialised-religious others and elsewheres. The Metropolitan Community Church

(MCC), founded in, by, and for the LGBTQ+ community, is a good example of community-led activism, families of choice, and do-it-yourself organising preceding supposedly progressive equality law. Yet MCC is often Christian and denominational by intention or effect, and UK MCC membership is likely to be overwhelmingly white. Like other religious organisations, MCC has stood in for state provisioning and made up for the shattered welfare system, with fundraising efforts becoming the norm rather than an emergency or crisis response. Yet faith-based communities are still often represented as innately stuck, rather than as creative or agentic, and as homophobic and hostile, with pink-washed Western liberal states now promoting their own progression and leadership through homonationalist showcasing.[26]

At the end of 2015 I returned to Scotland, following the independence referendum (2014), and paused on all the other places I'd called home since leaving Scotland in 2000. The political climate between then and now led me to wonder again about questions of being Scottish, British, and European, or not. In 2018 I began a comparative European project (including England, Germany, Portugal, and Scotland). During the fieldwork UK participants moved from being EU citizens to no longer being so, even if they felt and expressed themselves as still 'European'. EU citizens living in England and Scotland often found themselves entangled in bureaucracy, re-navigating citizenship rights, including welfare, employment, and residency. During this time, as before, I interviewed queer workers, residents, carers, parents, and citizens, as well as those without employment, those unable to gain work, those with pending asylum claims, and those who had changed their religion to, at least in part, become more of a fit with normative secular understandings of LGBTQ+ subjects. Overlapping with the global pandemic period, I interviewed NHS workers, lorry drivers, carers, key workers on the front line, furloughed workers, and those with families, cares, and communities in and beyond the new EU–UK boundaries. Some expressed a sense of loss of protection from 'Rainbow Europe', as a good ally for LGBTQ+ rights. Others never felt included or protected under such a rainbow and were keen to highlight class and racialised divisions in the accepted story of 'Rainbow Europe'. Scotland is implicated in this story as a 'wee', perhaps 'provincial', place taking up space, navigating its proximity to Europe and more globally, including in its claims to be a 'world leader' (of LGBTQ+ inclusion) and an exemplar of civic nationalism.

From 2020 to 2021 I held a visiting position as a Scottish Parliamentary fellow, researching 'COVID-19 and Lesbian, Gay, Bisexual, Trans (LGBT+) Life in Scotland'. Being sceptical of state inclusion, this might seem a strange place for me to situate myself; I did so pragmatically, while being ambivalent about policy reform or resolution. In pandemic times, certain populations were positioned again as at risk: resolving (ever-present) risk is also postponed, deferred to post-pandemic or post-crisis times (these times never arrive, due to the onset of other crises, and the continuation of economic crisis). The queer population reports inequalities in health, educational, employment, and social settings before, in and beyond pandemic times. In naming these realities over again in this book the intention is not to re-pathologise, exceptionalise, or homogenise. Social benefits and visibility are often afforded to those recognised as 'fitting' with standard depictions of family, domesticity, employability, and productivity. In contrast, some interviewees found it hard to access healthcare, including for fertility treatment or gender-affirming services. Others felt more surveilled or were living in circumstances which confounded the COVID-19 'stay at home' safety message. I have been re-energised by interviewees across present and past fieldwork, including ongoing LGBTQ+ forms of organising, which resonate and connect through lesbian, Black, queer, feminist activism (see Chapters 6 and 7).

Working-class, poor, and unemployed people, migrants, Black and minority ethnic people, disabled people, older people, and LGBTQ+ people stand out as repeatedly enduring crisis times. Working-class communities and individuals have been blamed for right-wing populism, racism, hetero-activism, and regressive Brexit fall-out, effectively excluding queers and/as people of colour from imaginings of the 'working class', and from everyday political progress, including just getting by in 'hostile environments'. Fighting for the queer left means more than accumulating legal entitlements within the nation state: we should be deeply suspicious about national governments as LGBT champions, and the conservatism limiting and undermining understandings of queer presences and politics, including its working-class formations:

> ... you know, somebody says working-class, we all visualise a white cis man with a flat cap and a whippet or whatever. I also think about how much that isn't actually what working-class communities think working-class is ... But all over the place were these, and not maiden aunts, they had bloody girlfriends that were living with them and long-term, and nobody talked about it ... And I think there's something for me about, even like in that generation, people kind of thirty, forty years older than me, queerness was quite visible. Like being working-class is queer.
>
> —Senior manager in UK LGBTQ+ organisation,
> interviewed 2021

THE QUEER CASE: CATEGORIES AND CASES

Working-Class Queers variously positions as a queer case study in several senses. Using fieldwork conducted over an extended period I *make a case* for the queer left across a 20-year period, covering New Labour to (post-)Brexit pandemic times. As an extended case, *Working-Class Queers* still navigates the disciplinary and normative framing and generalisability of *the case*: working-class queers may be imagined as few and far between, categorised in the 'other' sections of reading lists and imagined as a case apart (Chapters 2 and 7). In other words, there is already a case *against* working-class queers. In managing this, I also navigate the problem of too much data in making my case, while stretching the (social) scientific use of the case as proof, evidence, and positivistic truth. Social science disciplines think about the patterns between the singular and the generalisable, or the individual and the social, and in writing a book, this becomes a question of who will be selected and what work they will do for or against the general case.

Producing this book has necessarily meant prioritising some accounts over others. I haven't selected as a single or simple act, instead enacting correctives, interruptions, and repetitions in connecting cases and categories. The prevailing whiteness of the 'queer case' is challenged by including queers of colour and queer non-citizens, such as asylum seekers, those on work visas, and those who don't easily fit into local–national–international borders. Returning to un-used data, might un-do the research story told *then*, or might make evident the doing of stories *then and now* (Chapter 7). I make my case – as researcher, feminist, queer – in using other working-class queer cases, and these confirm and challenge each other ('case almost closed').

In being 'On the Case', Lauren Berlant[27] considers how the case represents a problem, hovering above 'the singular, the general, and the normative':

> ... to ask the question of what makes something a case, and not a merely gestural instance, illustration, or example, is to query the adequacy of an object to bear the weight of an explanation worthy of attending to and taking a lesson from; the case is actuarial ... To talk about someone or something as marked is to suggest that it is remarkable in itself but also that it is already strongly marked by exemplarity. Case almost closed: the marked subject is a walking exemplar, a person trailing an already-known story.

In selecting interviewees to variously represent 'working-class queers', I have paused on which cases count within that case, who can stand for the general and who gets us to a bigger place (when we are seen in, as, and from a 'wee place', see Chapters 4 and 5). Who is able to progress the pages of the book as they get stuck on other cases, such as the case of the individual white, middle-class, cis-het, able-bodied women generalisable as the 'everywoman' of feminism? Intersectionality has been invoked as the case for and against feminism – as 'still out of reach', as a failed yet returned-to theoretical and methodological drive. I use data extracts from transcripts, and I draw on more detailed accounts and experiences of particular interviewees who often don't make it into the case of queer-feminism, as an already-known versed story. This is a queer, intersectional effort where white, middle-class queerness is also interrogated rather than taken-for-granted. In selecting accounts beyond the 'walking exemplars' of feminist-queer studies, in this book I hope to generate other trails, re-doing and re-writing the case of working-class queers, as an '… event that takes shape'.[28] This book aims to be attentive to categories, as *the case* takes shape and as it in turn re-shapes queer-left politics and possibilities.

Chapter 1, 'Fighting for the Queer Left', has sought to contextualise writing, research and 'being working-class queer' across the long-term in relation to socio-political changes, where sometimes this has felt like 'crawling over glass'. Chapter 2, '(Un)Doing Queer-Class Data', considers what and who is 'left off' data collection and analysis, creating space for the data that sits at the margins of traditional parameters. Chapter 3, 'Queer Life in the Pandemic', persists with feminist queer-left thinking through pandemic times, focusing on race, class, and gender inequalities. Chapter 4, 'Queer Provincialisms in (Post-)Brexit Britain', asks what's at stake in state transformations and considers how this comes to matter for queers. Chapter 5, 'Queers and Austerity', turns back to research projects conducted across the decade-long period following the global financial crisis of 2008 and the onslaught of austerity. Chapter 6, 'Queer Anachronisms: Working-Class Lesbians out of Time and Place', looks back on 20 years of research on working-class lesbian lives in the UK to ask what lesbian studies can bring to our understanding of contemporary debates on real life at the intersection. Chapter 7, 'Towards a Queer Working-Class Reading List', positions re-reading in and through the changing queer-feminist classroom alongside my own entry points, from being a student to becoming a teacher. This is an ongoing, in many ways, uncompleted project, as the struggle in fighting for the queer left always is.

2

(Un)Doing Queer-Class Data

I volunteered to do it because I knew that there would probably be an under-representation of BAME participants in the project overall ... I don't volunteer for any qualitative interviews with people that I've not met before, or I don't know about them and their work.

—Alisha, 39, South Asian, lesbian

I feel a lot in my work, and maybe it is a sign of age as well, but I feel like I'm now in the cycle of repetition, that things that I said way back at the start ... But in terms of practice and moving forward, I noticed that [LGBT charity] has been doing a lot of things in terms of thinking intersectionally.

—Project worker, UK LGBT charity, interviewed 2021

As Alisha expresses, data is anticipated in calls for and responses from participants, and is always mediated, including as an exchange between the researcher and the researched, and between academic, popular, and policy circuits. Doing data is perhaps best imagined as participatory and responsive, embodied and carried in cycles of repetition.[1] Not dissimilar to LGBTQ+ organising and campaigning over a long-term period, I also repeat myself, with this repetition entangling academic projects, personal trajectories, and political climates. In committed, and even failing, repetitions, queer-class data is (un)done over time and across place: accessing 'hard to reach' populations may represent research success; situating ourselves reflexively vis-à-vis research respondents may represent sameness; and qualitative data might texture quantitative 'big data', through which marginalised groups repeatedly come to be known *as* and *at* risk. Certain groups are over-represented in and as dangerous or deficit data, known through income, educational, health, or employment statistics. In gathering data throughout a 20-year period of queer-feminist research, my persistent concern is one of mobilising data for social change.

I've interviewed over 250 people identifying as LGBTQ+ since 2001. This number amounts to a robust empirical sample, or to a significant 'dataset'. And yet the meanings, selections, edits, and returns to and through the data surpass any straightforward count or static archive: I count data as mattering in the context of social, cultural, and policy shifts, while also querying the categories invested in, reproduced, and shaken off (as 'working-class' and 'queer'). In going backwards–forwards over my data archive, I argue for the generative and transformative processes of *doing* data rather than just *being* data, as something that the queer left can reactivate. In revisiting data across time and place from different fieldwork contexts, I surpass my own count of x number of interviewees. I feel the embodied, politicised memories and presence of fieldwork: of hanging around, of meetings, emails, telephone calls, and conversations across time – of public space turned into ad hoc interview space, and of pages and pages of notes, diaries, and maps, which don't always fit neatly into the data archive (or funding repository).[2] I feel the continued pull of personal biography as political and generative, also attending to what is produced beyond myself. In this, I think with Alisha and others on the LGBTQ+ frontlines, about productive repetitions, participation, and 'coming forward' through our past and present positionings, as (un)doing data.

Alisha's account is suggestive of work still to do – and how this work might fall to *her* to come forward. Alisha volunteers in the social context of racism, knowing that as a Scottish South Asian lesbian she may be the only one in an otherwise white sample. She may be deemed 'hard to reach' and overlooked within sexualities research. Her transcribed words hint at efforts before and after the interview, as a moment of data capture or sample inclusion or participant voice and representation. White, middle-class, cis, gay men tend to be over-represented in sexualities research and an intersectional lens can be named, cited, aspired for – and yet be undone in practice.[3] In practice, I've tried to make space for under-represented LGBTQ+ participants, delaying responses and recruitment from 'go-to' groups (rather than filling up interview slots with those who come forward first and fast). Making and taking space potentially overlap and I've been conscious and cautious about over-recruiting, aware that more privileged LGBTQ+ interviewees have often (over)participated in research projects, becoming versed in interview questions, responses, and the right-to-speak. Categories can also contain and limit, glossing over their politicisation. Methodologically, intersectionality might enable attentiveness to samples and stories, as cases which trouble the usual go-to (even queer) scripts, confounding discrete measures or simple statistical truths, as 'protected characteristics'. The move to 'think intersectionally' means more than adding in 'Q' and '+' as to-be-included in the LGBT acronym now familiar and mainstreamed in policy formations.

As researchers we carry words, thoughts, feelings, and actions forward; we interrupt, stall, correct, and repeat ourselves, going back and forward with our interviewees, recruiting and returning to 'the field'. Nirmal Puwar explores embodied influences that weigh upon, surround, and encircle research practices and journeys, and in returning to Glasgow – and the Glasgow Women's Library (GWL) – I think about research relationships lived in and carried as 'obsessions, dreams and materials'.[4] Class and queer are written on and into the bodies of researchers, as 'archives of histories and labour',[5] and as more than academic deposit, baggage, or storage. I understand the question 'Where are you from?' as always loaded, and I share this load with research participants. We do not share this equally, however. One significant place 'where I'm (writing) from' is The University, which itself (un)does queer-class knowledges and practices, in producing data which 'counts'.

BEING DATA: 'WHERE ARE YOU FROM?'

Questions of identity can be risky, as the image in Figure 2.1 shows through contestation and erasure, even when intended as ethical practice, as in the case of data anonymisation. Nicola (21, white, gay, woman) pushed back at 'being data': asked if she had anything else to add to the interview, Nicola, in response to her assigned pseudonym, answered that '… my name is not "Nicola" (*laughter*)'.

Figure 2.1 and Figure 2.2 Images from 'Making Space for Queer-Identifying Religious Youth' research: 'You have taken away my identity' and 'Queer Identity and Religion' map.
Source: author's own images.

In her diary, the opening page reads 'You have taken my identity. How does this make me feel?', written below a drawing of a distressed, blindfolded face (Figure 2.1). Her mind map (Figure 2.2) is surrounded by personal nouns such as 'Friend', 'DYKE!', 'partner', 'Girlfriend', 'Granddaughter', as well as her real name. I am also invested in using real names, places, and experiences, such that the above extract causes pause as to who and what is (un)done in data and how data talks back and spills out of the archive. Here I tell part of my story, as I ask working-class queer interviewees to do, thinking about my own data entanglements. The questions 'who are you?', 'where are you from?', can pull us forward and push us back: I answer here, in part, by way of locating myself vis-à-vis my interviewees, readers, colleagues, and queers …

I'm from a working-class background. I say this in part to hold onto where I'm coming from – as a starting point rather than an end point or conclusion. I say I'm working class knowing that this still, always, provokes a reaction in the middle-class spaces that I now claim as mine. Being an academic wasn't the future my past self imagined for me, nor was it imagined by most of my school-teachers or family members – people from my estate never went to university. Yet I can say I'm a queer feminist professor. I can, and still, say I'm a working-class lesbian. Sometimes the saying and storying changes, depending on who is listening. Sometimes I say I'm from Glasgow. And sometimes it doesn't need to be said. Aware of the legitimations and interruptions to our 'own stories', I circulate mine with caution – knowing that it's already out there too, often 'outing' me before I open my mouth, and whether I sound authentically Glaswegian or not. In being in public – including in interview encounters – intimate judgements are made about where we are from, shared with and (un)done by interviewees:

… When I worked here I had that quite often, 'oh where are you from?', 'you have a very broad accent', 'I've never met anyone that talks like you before!' From somebody who says that they're from Edinburgh but they have a English accent. And I find that really peculiar, because there's a bit of like racism in there. Can I say racism? No, like hierarchies of accents.

—Dan, 36, white, gay, cis man, interviewed 2021

Sharon: I think we should try and stay in a working-class area to try and bring, to keep the standards up, you know. Try and keep it, I don't know what area in Glasgow you come from?

Yvette: Drumchapel.

Sharon: Within Glasgow there's very much pockets of deprivation. As soon as people get the chance to move out they should move out.

—Sharon, 47, white, lesbian, woman, interviewed 2001

As discussed with Sharon, I grew up in a Glasgow council estate called Drumchapel, built in the 1950s. According to Wikipedia – a public archive which can also circulate dangerous and deficit data – the area is a hub of social problems, with residents engaged in 'anti-social behaviour' from their 'poorly constructed post-war housing …'[6] On the one hand, this captures a truth encapsulated in a G15 postcode – housing conditions were often substandard, and I have no nostalgia for 'poorly constructed' council houses, viewing the provision of decent and affordable housing as necessary and urgent. On the other hand, I'm sceptical about how affordability or liveability has come to constitute another opportunity for regeneration, privatisation, and failure, while individual tenants are either applauded or condemned for engaging in the Right to Buy[7] scheme. As tenants – and in my gran and granda's case, lifelong ones since the building of the estate – no one in my family could exercise their 'right to buy', and I'm ambivalent about apportioning praise or blame in this reality. As a young person I became familiar with standing in queues at the housing and benefits office, watching my mum, and many others, plead for a crisis allowance, a clothing grant, a council house swap. And I felt the judgements from local authority administrators and bureaucrats up close and personal, not just as representations or discourses.

I left Glasgow – and specifically Drumchapel – in 1996, and I left Scotland in 2000. In these moves the shape of class and queer both changed and remained: Scotland often represents itself as entirely working-class, by virtue of its supposed down-to earth, say-it-like-it-is non-pretentiousness, and often as a claim of cross-border difference from England and Englishness (see Chapter 4).

Deindustrialised cities like Glasgow undoubtedly have deep-seated problems – even named as 'The Glasgow Effect' – yet when pitched as a local or even national story, the rise and demise of Glasgow's industries can disguise a wider implicatedness in global chains of production and exploitation: the industrial past can be lamented, as a loss for white working-class men, effacing the ongoing effects of colonial legacies in the present.[8] Scotland has recently emphasised civic nationalism over ethnic nationalism (see Chapter 4), and Glasgow in particular has shown support for refugees and asylum seekers. Slogans such as 'refugees welcome here' and the term 'Refuweegee' – combining 'weegie',[9] as a person from Glasgow, with 'refugee' – have been popularised and politicised, beyond the charity ('Refuweegee') of the same name. The charity's website declares that 'We're all fae somewhere', again mixing the local and global. But this mix arguably stands in contrast to the reality of Scotland as overwhelmingly white. The 2011 Census found that:

- Scotland's population was 96.0 per cent white, a decrease of 2.0 per cent from 2001;
- 91.8 per cent of people identified as 'White: Scottish' or 'White: Other British';
- 4.2 per cent of people identified as Polish, Irish, Gypsy/ Traveller or 'White: Other';
- the population in Asian, African, Caribbean or Black, Mixed or Other ethnic groups doubled to 4 per cent.

Scottish cities are constituted differently, and in 2011, 17.3 per cent of Glasgow's population identified as an ethnic minority – including 2.4 per cent as White: Other, 1.9 per cent as White: Irish, and 1.4 per cent as White: Polish.[10] Dan's struggle to navigate the classed question of 'where are you from?' turned into a question about where your *accent* is from, resonating with the racialisation of such questions and codes. Dan conflates and then self-corrects and differentiates between not having an Edinburgh accent and being subject to racism ('No, like hierarchies of accents'). Being local and being welcomed into the 'local' space can feel like being data, whether exceptional, too small to count, too provincial, or as part of a big, expanded city bracket ('Weegie') and different, civic nation state.

Scotland has implemented various race equality policies,[11] whilst also seeing an increase in racism as a reported hate crime. As everyday patterns, 'micro-aggressions', 'casual racism', and 'everyday sexism' persist across places. Living in England and returning to Scotland has meant living through and witnessing these familiar and persistent patterns, rather than moving away from them. In moving between Scotland and England, I don't necessarily or automatically feel 'at home' in my natal city of Glasgow where I now work. Feeling this way as part of a re-valuation of what citizenship, community, and belonging looks like in central and peripheral parts of the UK in changing times is not the same as feeling forced out. I continue to correct, when England and Englishness stands in for UK-wide, and in a moment of Brexit Britain I'm keen to note that Scotland didn't vote for Brexit.

But I'm also keen to note that many parts of England didn't either.[12] English colleagues in the Scottish workplace sometimes defer, sometimes celebrate – they moved north 'at the right time'; they don't know that word, accent, or term, but will eagerly learn soon! In these movements back and forward, I don't always know if my own movements or words are local, national, or international, but I do imagine that this is a story about class as much as it is about nationality. I've felt class divisions within Scotland, and in daily interactions, housing conditions, educational systems, and (un)employment realities. Growing up poor in Scotland, being from the wrong part of a Scottish city, means being sceptical about borders, even when cast as better borders. It means being sceptical about words and phrases, once corrected at school, and now rolled off the tongue as humour, capital, and claim.

My return to the local context, as a Glaswegian, implicates and entwines the global – as travel, mobility, escape, homecoming. At the end of 2015 I returned to Scotland – from being generically Scottish in London to possibly being known specifically as from *there*, an awkward Wikipedia entry judging and returning me home. Now living in Scotland, my accent has changed again, and I'm often asked where I'm from. Asking and answering feels like dis-connection, revelation, and confirmation. In trying to subvert or refuse the question, I still sense where the conversation is going, as I know the usual patterns and embodiments that are traced as go-to stories. 'Where are you from?', colleagues ask, potentially seeking common ground, even as we dance around our respective locations with embarrassment and even apologies (disclosing middle-class residency can also embarrass!). Where I'm from can be evidenced as authenticity of working-classness or as indicative of escape and the possibility of becoming middle-class. I've been invoked as the story of mobility in educational outreach contexts ('Yvette's from Drumchapel!'), and I know that being local might have purchase, as others are never seen as entitled to such a claim. I've been asked if, and how many, relatives 'still live there'. I've wondered about what is really being asked: if relatives, like me, 'got out'; if I awkwardly go-between 'separate worlds'; or if invoking people in place still ultimately mis-places us? In negotiating these distances, I'm careful about the question 'where are you from?' and whether to return it, as postcodes become predictive data.

Postcodes place pupils in school 'catchment areas' as early predictors of possibilities. I began school in 1983, just before the introduction of Section 28 (in 1988) banning the 'promotion of homosexuality as a pretended family relationship', enacted by the Thatcher Conservative government. In 2018 I held a workshop to think through the impact and enduring legacies of Section 28, with participants' postcards carrying these through time:

To Margaret Thatcher... A better person than me would write that I forgive you, and that I admire you as a woman who became leader. But I do not forgive or admire you. You used your place of privilege to remove the human rights of a generation and set back the cultural development of a whole country. So there is no admiration, but also no resentment. Just deep disappointment. What a terrible disappointment to us all you were Margaret.

To Margaret Thatcher... My grandfather used to hope for your death. I was extra-sad that you outlived him – not only because I had fewer years with him, but because the world had more years with you. Because more beautiful working-class, POC and LGBTQ people were made miserable by you, died because of you. I raise a glass to my grandfather on your death day. And to everyone else who deserved so much more.

To Margaret Thatcher... you lost.

—Postcards from workshop, 2018: 'To Margaret Thatcher ...'

The Thatcherite era also saw a wave of rebranding rundown cities, with Glasgow becoming increasingly positioned as 'vibrant' and attractive, as witnessed in the much-cited 'Glasgow's Miles Better' campaign. But this didn't reach Drumchapel. The material and the moral circulated in everyday places, in the council estate, in the school, between peers, friends, and teachers. My mum gave me a special name, and my primary class was similarly populated with 'unusually named' children, which teachers often remarked on and laughed at. I look back as an adult and see the usual teachers placing and sorting the unusual children in the usual classed ways. Perhaps like other parents, my mum wanted me to be a different child even as I traced her steps in going to the same school she'd gone to. She told me I had 'dolly mixture' eyes, perhaps as another way to feel special and different – and the teacher laughed for a long time when I confidently declared this (my eyes are green). The kinds of buffers that working-class parents put in place to enable their kids to get-by, rather than get-on socially or educationally, are rarely praised. I knew my family was different – and even different to other working-class families within the same council estate – as my mum was a young single parent, and in the '80s this stigma was still felt sharply. In being official dangerous data, measured in low life expectancy, educational failure, and teenage pregnancy rates, working-class parents nonetheless refuse judgements and re-invest in working-class parenting as more caring and less socially harmful:

I do want her [daughter] to finish her education, I do want her to get a steady career and if she wants to have a family, have a family, if not then have a nice, stable life for herself, you know? I don't want her to mess around with her life, I don't want her to sort of get into trouble 'cause that's kinda what I did when I was younger. I left high school really early on, I moved out of my mam's home when I was 16 and I got my own place and I kinda struggled to get by. I don't want her to do that. I hope that she learns from my mistakes not to kinda dwindle her life away and just try to do the best for herself, whatever that may be. I mean if your best is working in McDonald's and you know, then that's fine by me so long as she does to her full potential that's all I really care about.

—Karen, 22, white, lesbian, interviewed 2009

The other day when I was at my work, I was outside at the food bank and when the bus passed by and it was like 'Is your son ready for private school?' ... I found that I couldn't help myself looking at the kid and thinking 'You're going to be a fucking Tory MP or something'.

—Lewis, 29, white, pansexual, gender queer, interviewed 2021

By the 1990s, I'd somehow caught a teacher's eye, and was earnestly told to 'Escape Drumchapel!', propelling me eastwards to Edinburgh. Yet as an undergraduate at an elite Russell Group university, I felt and knew class even more, and was unsure if I was in fact escaping at all. I knew class in its various forms: as the surprise that someone from an infamous council estate would go to university; as the end of the student maintenance cheque and the non-payment of rent; as hardship fund applicant made to confess their poverty as poor management; and as a loud 'local' voice then tuned down in tutorials, responding to looks, glances, and giggles. I juggled part-time work, which was nearer full-time hours, being a lucky recipient of a full Student Awards Agency Scotland (SAAS) maintenance grant. The promise of mobility fell short then, as it does now in an era of tuition fees, meaning that working-class students now increasingly stay with their families, and attend local institutions (having a rather different 'student experience'). Dan's (36, white, gay cis man) reminder that '... not everybody's followed that. Not everybody went to university or left their hometown or their home locality and lived this gay life', is an important one. 'Going to Yale to be a Lesbian'[13] (or going to Edinburgh) is mocked because of its pretentiousness, and because of the performativity and materiality in going places:

> If you'd asked me ... 'How long have you got until you go to university?' I could tell you the exact number of days ... I just *had* to get to university. Then as soon as I waved my parents off ... and I was like, 'argh' and all these emotions sort of just came out and it was interesting. So yes, and then as soon as I got to university, I'd go to church and because I didn't feel like I fitted in because there was something not quite right, it was the sort of 'gay' trying to get out and I just didn't feel like I fitted in.
>
> —Nicola, 21, white, gay, woman, interviewed 2011

> So, you know, I remember, possibly what I remember first of all is, when I came to Glasgow School of Art, I mean I couldn't believe that I'd got in. I was like 'oh my god this is amazing', and I thought, wrongly, that it would be a kind of, you know, bastion of liberalism and kind of really cool kind of lefty people, and it wasn't that at all. I mean it was homophobic, racist, sexist, I mean sexual harassment. And so I remember I did my dissertation for my final year on Section 28 and you had to kind of present on that. And my department actually they were cool, they all knew me, so, you know, I was out and everything to them.
>
> —Sally, 56, white, lesbian, interviewed 2020

My own entrance to higher education was in between Sally's and Nicola's, and none of us felt overly nostalgic about university. But I felt part of a new and different city, one I'd never even been to before, even though it's situated less than 50 miles from Glasgow. It was exciting, a big escape, and only when hearing of bigger, longer distances traversed by other students did I feel local and small. I queued up every year to collect my cheque upon matriculating, which also required a meeting with my tutor. For me, these meetings were reminiscent of receiving the free school dinner ticket and feeling a mix of shame, entitlement, anger, and satisfaction. On one occasion while waiting for my tutor, I overheard his loud conversation, complete with joyful laughter: another student was recounting stories of summer holidays and skiing; there was no urgency and their ten-minute appointment lapsed into 20 minutes, then 30. I waited patiently through her tales, then eventually knocked loudly on the door, shouting 'I need to pick up my grant!', bursting with frustration. They looked at one another and nervously laughed. He signed off my form with none of the same pleasantries that they'd shared.

From the corridor to the classroom, I was the wrong kind of student. I changed seminar groups at least once because all the other students were what was described then, and likely still now, as upper-class 'yahs'. I literally couldn't get a word in edgeways, past the yahs. Eventually I stopped trying and just glared and seethed. Tutors would laugh and refer to the 'wee quiet Scottish lasses', as if they were a distinct personality, instead of a distinct positioning and politics – perhaps the only way to cope with stifling middle-upper-class environments, where students already knew their destinies and exuded the full confidence that afforded them. As an undergraduate, I knew class outside and inside of the classrooms and corridors. I felt and knew it in the LGBT Student Society, which I attended once and made a sharp exit from, knowing that I didn't belong there either, however highly the university ranked in LGBT charity Stonewall's 'Gay by Degree' data on good gay institutions.[14]

The library seemed a space I could fit into, find a corner. I found Bev Skeggs' book *Formations of Class and Gender*,[15] and it resonated with the hard work of care that I did throughout my undergraduate, and later postgraduate, degrees, working as a care assistant with an agency, often doing sleepovers where I'd get no sleep, rolling into tutorials the next day. Tutors frowned, sighed, and assumed I was reluctant, impolite, and hungover. Agency care work took me in and out of people's homes across the class spectrum and beyond the go-to university centre, while the nursing home I worked in – walking away from university in my ill-fitting and distinctly un-queer pink uniform – was located in an affluent suburb. I developed a sense that even middle- and upper-class existences could be rendered precarious, troubled by declining mental and physical health – and troubled too by a 19-year-old getting by and sometimes failing at caring. Families, it seemed, often didn't care. This seemed distinctly different and more neglectful than the way

my family really didn't care much about me going to university –
as unremarkable, rather than wilfully ignored. A queerer sense of
what and who counts as families grew here, too, as it developed
in my undergraduate and postgraduate feminist classrooms. My
head spun at the possibilities of adding 'with Gender Studies' to
my otherwise straitlaced Politics degree – I did so with joy and
rage, emboldened again by feminist academics that the 'personal
was political', that care was work, and that class, gender, and sexuality were structures, terms, and meanings through which I
could understand and re-shape my own experiences. I found

Figure 2.3   Location of Glasgow Women's Library, 1994–2007.[16]
Source: author's image.

feminism in – and often in spite of – my undergraduate experiences, and it became a way to think through different entries into and exits from academia and what could be carried inside–outside.

Universities are not the only place of being and doing data – community education ventures and venues do so too, often as politicised outreach projects. Through time, Glasgow Women's Library (GWL)[17] has functioned as that kind of venue for me, from being a young person and user of its services, to an academic hosting events, to introducing university students to its library, and to donating resources to support a broader learning community. GWL – like the feminist reading list, like the (un)doing of data – allows an opening back and forward through these weighted, embodied issues. But only if we read, action, and activate the messy contents as practice and work, as *doing* data.

DOING DATA: QUEER/CLASS

Regional divides	Equality	Pride
Education	Public schools	Student Grants
Scotland	USA	Common
Crime rates	Publics	Estates
Ireland	India	Hate Crime
Precarity	Privilege	Minimum wage
Dole	Debt	Family credit
Rainbows	#BLM	Job Centre
Labour	Royals	Snobby
Lesbian Avengers	Precarity	Mutual Aid
Social Distance	Furlough	South Africa
Spain	Drugs	Mental Health
HIV/AIDS	Pandemic	Prison
COVID-19	Intersectionality	Names – Karen
#Covidiots	#LwiththeT	Free Pride
Hierarchy	QueerCrip	GRA
Identity	Feminism	Charity
Welfare	Intersectionality	#MeToo
Libraries	TERFS	Section 28
DATA	Racism	

—Glasgow Women's Library, Queer/Class words listed in
Queer/Class Workshop, March 2020

Being at Glasgow Women's Library (GWL) represents a return to one of my formative queer sites, acting as a reminder of being and doing queer data across the long-term. The GWL's *Poverty and Social Exclusion of Lesbians and Gay Men in Glasgow* report[18] from the late 1990s inspired my own postgraduate academic journey, angrily motivating me: on the front page the authors and library co-founders declare that 'lesbians and gay men are ... marginalised, depressed, skint, bullied, homeless, sick, unsupported, selling sex, unemployed, poor, assaulted, victimised, discriminated against, silenced, bored'. In returning to Scotland in 2015 I went back to the relocated GWL Lesbian Archive: I saw *Working-Class Lesbian Life* on the bookshelf and thought again about being and doing data as an ongoing working-class queer (project). The above list co-produced as part of a Queer/Class workshop held at GWL in 2020, just before the UK lockdown, is one of opportunities, experiences, and connections. The workshop event also celebrated the launch of Matt Brim's *Poor Queer Studies* (2020),[19] as a welcome corrective to 'rich queer studies', filtered and streamed through elite institutions. In organising the event, I wanted to think through and with the communities that I'd spent time in, been a member of, interviewed, and researched over decades. Much of the above list could have been reproduced in 2000 or 2010 or 2020, a circular feedback loop of making space.

But even when written down, these lists can become discarded rather than considered evidence of queer–class intersection. Some things don't become categorised or archived on the library shelves, even when produced in a library, as this one was – and sometimes not even when co-produced with academics. We were welcomed into the workshop event, told about the possibilities of collecting, depositing and archiving, of making knowledge in and through feminist spaces ('we want your stuff, we want to archive all this, and we're going to put a general call out to make sure that we can get this stuff together'). But sometimes general calls, to produce, know, and list, don't produce transformation, but rather more of the same, as standard go-to lists, matching words, codes, and categories. After the event I'm handed a gift, a smooth pebble engraved with 'In the hands of the proletariat', and I turn it over in my hands

Figure 2.4   Glasgow Women's Library, Queer/Class workshop, 2020, 'In the hands of the proletariat'.

Source: author's image.

and wonder about the smooth surface appeal, against the weight of the terms: whose hands, which proletariat?

GWL has taken a long time to materialise in its now secure permanent location, in the working-class area of Bridgeton, having been precariously rehoused over the years, including in central, if temporary accommodation, at the prestigious and celebrated Mitchell Library. Having hosted events at GWL over the years, I've been cautioned about that 'part of town', assumed to be doing 'outreach'. Some say that Bridgeton is a more accessible place, not far from the train station, and open to different communities. Difference is often coded as deficit, a euphemism that means this is not quite the right place, or containing the right people. Relocating to Bridgeton signals the competing recognition and resourcing of 'women's issues', where intersectionalities are worked into – and out of – the bricks and mortar of buildings and communities, as well as in library book pages.

As it states on its website, GWL is the only Accredited Museum in the UK dedicated to women's lives, histories, and achievements, with a lending library, archive collections, and innovative programmes of public events and learning opportunities. The library is not just a library, but also a museum, a learning hub, a community venue, and so much more; it's not just local (Glasgow), but internationally recognised; and it is not just for cis women, operating a trans and non-binary inclusive policy. It might be a queer

Figure 2.5 Glasgow Women's Library Archive, photographed 2019.

Source: author's image.

space. This site still feels new for me, with my past memories of it as an obviously precarious space (see Figure 2.3, showing the GWL's location, 1994–2007), bolstered by the efforts of founding staff and a host of volunteers. It may still be a precarious space, just missing out on being awarded Museum of the Year, and likely still subject to funding application failures, and successes.

I opened the workshop by 'situating myself'. In sharing my intention wasn't just to authenticate my own story. My story of queer-class is not the only, or best, story, and I told it not to nec-essarily prove that I am ultimately working-class, or to cement a binary between working-class and middle-class lives (although often this is enacted as a material divide with blunt edges). The same can go for queer and straight lives. We are not only knowable via our class-queer positions, as intersections which surpass stories or identity declarations in LGBTQ+ 'outness'. This was made vivid in the example which author and guest speaker Matt Brim invoked in introducing his book *Poor Queer Studies*. Expand-ing on an example from his book, he explained the three-hour commute which one of his students, a young Black lesbian, took daily to attend university at a distance from her Harlem neigh-bourhood. By travelling across distances she can be 'out', but live 'local' and still afford to go to university. Rather than presenting this as a sad tale, only to be reconciled by 'getting out', away from her neighbourhood via credentialised university education, a more complicated tale of opportunity, agency, and constraint was woven into class–queer intersectionality.

As an example of data gathered and real lives lived, this is a familiar story. It is one of possibilities, and impossibilities, of negotiating differently classed terrain, of going back and forward, round and round, to find opportunities, and to afford the train fare. Much of the data, meanings, people, conversations, stories, laughter, and tears that I've gathered, met, heard, and shared over the years in interviewing working-class queers, has demonstrated this and more: being stuck, not getting out, not attending university, and not finding employment. I only had to think back to who wasn't in the room. But the stories of class and queerness are multiple and messy, confounding easy 'lost girl' or 'girl makes good' exemplars. In the Queer/Class workshop we heard from someone who taught modern languages but confounded the usual imagination of a mobile queer citizen: she was anxious and unable to raise the issue of LGBTQ+ inclusion in the workplace, a school, because of her temporary status. Outness, or Pride, can stop and stall when the risk is unemployment, particularly when UK Brexit means that EU citizens, welcomed here to teach UK children other languages, are viewed with suspicion. Equality and diversity issues are separated – linguistic appeal counterposed against sexual-gender-cultural excess – yet embodied in workers, participants, and friends. Another participant, a non-native (at least bilingual) English speaker, struggled to make his point about the inaccessibility of language, and what, and who, counts – and was spoken over.

We spoke over each other and wrestled again with what, and who, matters more; class displaced gender, and gender displaced race. Such accounting and displacement never sounds very queer, as a stretch beyond singular categories and identities, or equal opportunity boxes. One participant was all but shut down when raising issues of race and the racialised aspects of belonging in Scotland (but read many, or any, places).

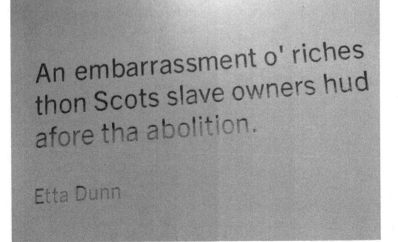

An embarrassment o' riches thon Scots slave owners hud afore tha abolition.

Etta Dunn

Figure 2.6 Glasgow Women's Library, Queer/Class workshop, 2020, Inscription on table.
Source: author's image.[20]

Figure 2.7   Glasgow Women's Library, Queer/Class workshop, 2020, 'Equal opportunities' box.

Source: author's image.

Another took the circulating white guilt on as hers; her South African nationality was presented as an admission, perhaps allowing others off the hook. One participant came out as a straight, married, Muslim woman who experienced racism in the 'People Make Glasgow'[21] city. The university did little to materially alleviate her homelessness as a result of her landlord's racism; she was wholly imagined as a privileged international student where emergency accommodation was reserved for a more local student, more easily imagined as worthy. Institutional practices and responses, including those framed as 'widening participation', can work to gloss over more complicated, globalised intersections of race, class and gender. Others talked about the precarity of their employment, of changing accents and feeling out-of-place, of not going to celebrated LGBTQ+ bars, and, as queers, of avoiding working-class places, venues, and pubs. Some people talked about fearing landlords' rent hikes and push-outs, as UK lockdown looked imminent – and later became a reality. There was some discomfort in our (un)willingness to name places we would not go, as words like 'rough', 'ned', and 'chav' also slipped in. The prevailing sectarian frame cutting across Glasgow's image of itself was quickly side-stepped. Those initially unfamiliar with the specific local terms, histories, and presences, quickly caught on nonetheless: whatever the words, the affects circulate – even within working-class communities, even within queer communities. The now international GWL, with its proud flag signalling award-winning nominations, was inhabited awkwardly, with some of us bumping up against its working-class Bridgeton neighbours. Multiple neighbouring pubs were named as obvious no-go areas for queers, while some queers immediately moved towards these places on exiting.

Having gathered, returned to, and recirculated some of my own data (including as 'academic', 'queer', 'Glaswegian', 'feminist', and so on), I move to what and who is 'left off' or carried through field-work and analysis. Creating space for data that sits at the margins of traditional parameters can become the stuff of 'obsession and dreams' even in times of enduring crisis.

3

Queer Life in the Pandemic

@YvetteTayloro What has been the impact of the COVID-19 pandemic on LGBT+ people and communities in Scotland? See Scottish Parliamentary Information Centre blog @ SPICe_Research[1]

@notneeded Can I have those 4 minutes back please? And just how much ££££ did she/her #NewSNP ScotGov supply? Maybe you can undertake research into why that nasty virus doesn't recognise how special you think LGBT people are. The nerve of it - infecting them!!

—Twitter exchange, 2021

Figure 3.1 Postcard image completed by interviewees, 2020–22.

As a queer-feminist researcher I'm compelled by what queer life in the pandemic is, and how crisis contexts persist as social epidemics. In 2020–21 I took up a parliamentary fellowship on the intersectional impact of COVID-19 on LGBTQ+ people, asking 'what has queer life in the pandemic been like?' I did so in response to the crisis, as part of my normal salaried academic duties, and as part of a long-term feminist commitment to making a difference and engaging with policy and practice. Ongoing engagements rarely translate into policy change or state reform. I'm fully aware that my limited-to-700-words blog post, timed as a four-minute read, is insufficient. I pause on word counts, Twitter characters, and headlines as I'm asked to fit my report abstract into 50 words, which simply stated:

> This briefing looks at the impact of COVID-19 on Lesbian, Gay, Bisexual, Trans (LGBT+) Life in Scotland. It draws on current literature and qualitative research to describe intersecting impacts across social, cultural and economic life. Commitments to LGBT+ equality can be productively embedded in post-pandemic recovery plans.

In between sentences as bullet points, the + sneaked into the standard LGBT parliamentary-approved acronym. In reporting back, I stated that politicians and policy makers '… may wish to detail and expand upon usage, particularly in relation to other minoritised positions such as asexual, intersex, and non-binary identities. Academic and activist research often uses "Queer" as an umbrella term encompassing non-heterosexual identities, and often highlighting broader non-normative positions.' The question of what and who counts is one I have considered on a long-term basis, having been named and placed as useless, diversionary, fraudulent, over-privileged, complicit, and costly. Doing research in, by, and for LGBTQ+ communities has long been viewed as singular or suspicious, as a 'special' interest, bias, or overstated claim, wrongly diverting resources from *real* causes. We can be publicly and professionally (un)done but doing fieldwork during a pandemic has returned me to questions of what matters and what to do in and through these new-old conditions.

I read hostility, affront, and queerphobia in the above Tweet: 'The nerve of it – infecting them!' Even as statistics are collated it is not clear whether LGBTQ+ people are considered fully within what counts, imagined still as deficits or excesses, medicalised as 'at risk', or mainstreamed as 'normal' consumers, parents, and workers. These predictable patterns intersect with heightened racism and the racialised naming of COVID-19 strains embedded within the search for the origins of the pandemic. A generalised 'hostile environment' abounds, while individual kindness is pitched as cure and congratulated. In the UK we clapped for the NHS, trying to cure systematic exploitation and underfunding with applause. This chapter frames queer life in and beyond the pandemic as an intersectional effort, surpassing individual frustrations or nerves: it thinks through the challenges of being and doing queer life within pandemic and endemic crisis contexts. The odds of survival, of securing a future or a 'liveable life',[2] continue to weigh in favour of the already advantaged: minoritised ethnic people, older people, those with disabilities and care responsibilities, and those precariously employed and unemployed, bear a disproportionate burden as the enduring crisis of our times.

KEY-QUEER WORKERS?

I urge you at this moment of national emergency to stay at home, protect our NHS and save lives.

—Boris Johnson, March 2020[3]

Yes, I'm working-class, I'm queer but then I'm not too sure about the British point, because I haven't been here for quite long enough.

—Jaslene, 37, South East Asian, lesbian

Seeing the poster call for participants, Jaslene had hesitated over the criteria and whether she fitted into what I wanted or expected ('But then I was thinking "why not just give it a try?" It's not going to hurt!'). Her hesitation and full interview account challenges ideas of what constitutes class and who can become, or be recognised as, 'working-class' in the UK. Jaslene raises the question about the 'British point', which often becomes a sharply excluding point – a point of being recognisable, or properly working-class. Working-classness is often imbued with whiteness, with heroic working communities of the past racialised by a white-washed remembering, and a forgetting of the imperialist economies at the centre of global class-making. The contemporary UK working-class is often imagined as white, despite repeated studies on the enduring linkages between ethnicity and poverty, and the histories of nation-building relying on mobilising racialised workers.[4] Jaslene's pause must become a collective pause and politicisation where the categories of class (and queer) are already narrowly constructed as 'British' or 'Western'. Such a status may still be denied to Jaslene, despite her residency, as not 'long enough' and as bound to visa requirements. However long Jaslene stays in the UK the category of working-class is likely to be misrecognised as only referring to a white population: Jaslene's circumstances question these common go-to references and associations of class and how it translates across borders. These circumstances become more than individual conditions or exceptions, thoroughly structured as they are through the global reproduction of inequalities, including in times of 'national emergency', and as this continues through climate crisis, energy crisis, recession, and the cost-of-living crisis. The comfort of 'staying at home', as a public health message which Boris Johnson invoked throughout the pandemic, is questionable in the context of escalating and unaffordable domestic costs.

Staying 'at home' is not available to Jaslene, where she does not have easy access to either the UK or the Philippines as homes, even as she works to 'save the NHS'. Discriminatory conditions – of welfare in crisis, of global workers welcomed in and pushed out, of regional, national, and international health disparities – persisted even as NHS workers were applauded during the first wave of the pandemic, and even as those claps ended. Black, Asian and minority ethnic (BAME) doctors and nursing staff were among the first to die of COVID-19, disproportionately impacted throughout, including via personal protective equipment (PPE) shortages.[5]

As someone on a sponsored visa with conditions pending renewal, Jaslene's wages are deliberately depressed to below the UK average pay for nurses. When her full nursing registration comes through she will receive a marginally higher salary on the bottom rung of the pay scale (and still well below the UK median).[6] Her salary is shared with her family in the Philippines, and she related how she spent money only on food and rent: 'I think they're thinking "Oh you've got much money, can you send some!" (laughs) that's kinda part of Philippine culture. When you are single, it's either that, or you send for your brothers and sisters, or for your parents, or for family members.' Jaslene's class belonging may be difficult to trace or understand in the context of migration but only if class positioning is separated from, rather than seen as constituted through, global chains of care and capitalism. Pursuing a nursing career in the UK, when her preferred USA route via a nursing programme proved more challenging, was not freely chosen. Jaslene's employment choices must be situated within a broader frame implicating her family, and the expectations around upward mobility and migrancy, which bumped against isolation, workplace discrimination, low pay in the public sector, and the challenges of being an essential worker during a global pandemic.

At the time of the interview, Jaslene was working long shifts and navigating care for COVID-19 patients often without PPE. She was resigned to this pressure, with no feasible alternative, and talked about mask re-usage, being provided with no or limited supplies, and caring for people with coronavirus who'd simply been moved into a corner room ('If there's a suspected COVID patient and we're still waiting for the results then they're being put in a side room'):

.... Whenever we go into the side room that's the only time we can wear masks and aprons and gloves ... there was a point when I didn't want to go to work because I think the procedures in place are not enough and it's likely to cause more infections. It's been scary. There are people in self-isolation, some are symptomatic so they have to stay at home ... that means there are less people at work, so it adds to the stress.

Promises of state reform wear thin, and extensions of visas for international NHS workers don't become an acknowledgement of collective vulnerabilities and inter-dependencies, but rather an arrogant framing of extended invites, to save 'us', the British public. It was under such conditions, within the UK's hostile environment,[7] that Jaslene persisted. Jaslene was actively recruited to the UK on the promise of better employment. Her employment, as a nurse, has always been precarious, rather than preferred or easily chosen. Jaslene did not want to be a nurse in the UK and, like her international peers housed in shared accommodation, this represented a typical story – one of weighing up possibilities rather than a queer story of escape from given to chosen family, or from rural to urban locales.

Her (dis)location represented queer particularity and precarity across race and class: she described living with an international group of nurses in simple residences and forming her own modest mutual aid group as a necessary yet understated practice. In describing shared meals, turn-taking, rotating the use of collective spaces, such everyday cares seemed under-recognised, and did not seem to be what was named or known by loud, proud mutual aid groups, variously engaged in creating, claiming, and naming the LGBTQ+ community, including through successful 'GoFundMe' campaigns. Instead, Jaslene and her peers, friends, and housemates often did these things in and as silences: not saying how homesick its members were, not making a noise in the knowledge that someone else would be sleeping close by, and not naming the failure of the LGBTQ+ community, or workplace dissatisfaction, or experiences of exclusion in the UK, as not quite what was promised or expected ... In other words, Jaslene could be described as living with 'quiet Pride' (as named by another respondent later in this chapter).[8]

Jaslene had a mixed experience of living and working in the UK's NHS and spoke of feeling isolated in many different ways because she was queer, working-class, an essential worker, and a migrant. She desperately missed her family, and had returned to the Philippines about once a year before COVID-19 travel restrictions made this difficult. But Jaslene lives through the consequences of not seeing family as her *long-term* reality. Her sporadic visits back to the Philippines involved much joy and upset, knowing her job would call her back to the UK. Her careful plans and budgeting had been disrupted and limited via country 'traffic-light' systems, which saw the Philippines in the red list 'restricted countries' category. Although Jaslene had friends and colleagues in similar positions, she was unwilling to talk about her feelings with them, keen not to displace her upset onto them in sharing the reality of distance between work and family life:

> I just cry my eyes out. I can never get used to leaving home, I can never get used to leaving people, I don't know if only I could bring them here. I mean I can make do with video calls and video chat but then there's my dog and he doesn't really look at the camera! (laughs) ... Most of my friends here, when it comes to culture, they're living on their own away from family and they might not understand it. With my fellow Filipino nurses, I wouldn't want to say because I know that they'll miss home, so I don't need to tell them about it. I know they might have their own problems and suffering.

Jaslene experienced workplace conflict but was reluctant to name this directly as racism – phrasing it instead as 'cultural' or 'linguistic' difference as she talked around it. I read racism into her story even as she drew away from that term – or drew away from using it in front of me as a white researcher, perhaps knowing that I might turn her pain into my white-guilt.[9] Instead, Jaslene expressed that she, herself, hadn't and wasn't absorbing the 'right' UK 'culture' or terms. She was often read as too direct, abrupt and harsh in the workplace, and I paused on the contrast between what I was seeing in a careful and considerate interviewee, willing to give up her time post-workshift, against a supposedly angry worker, made to feel she didn't fit in, despite all her work. Jaslene smiled throughout her interview, laughing and joking and, again, repeating a familiar embodied pattern: despite stories of struggle, interviewees often smiled and dismissed these same issues as not mattering, or at least not very much. Jaslene understood that she might be misrecognised as inarticulate, even rude and angry, and that she would have to adjust to this: 'So I need to adjust how I say it. I'm used to talking in English but it's different from the usual way of saying it back home. Here it would sound blunt and a bit rude, that's what they would say (laughs).' Being a queer woman of colour may always mean standing out and being seen as blunt and rude.[10] Jaslene is not a fully entitled or legitimate citizen, even as she performs and enacts the very service that the entitled British public demands. In ending our interview, our conversation turns to Jaslene's next shift and the hope that it might be better than the last: these are the small, everyday commitments often glossed over in national proclamations of 'our NHS', as held up by others.

The NHS may be queered by LGBTQ+ workers, and queer individuals and groups may make various claims and demands on it, including as entitled citizens. The headline 'How Long Can the NHS and Queer Community Share the Rainbow Flag?'[11] captured the feelings expressed by many interviewees during periods of UK lockdown, that the rainbow flag as a symbol of LGBTQ+ pride and community had been appropriated and depoliticised as a happy symbol for a (broken) NHS. However, this tension highlights a glossing-over of queer-classed realities.

Jaslene's stress as an NHS worker from the Philippines, working with COVID-19 patients, *and* working through longer-term health and social crises, is not one foregrounded in homogeneously highlighting LGBTQ+ people as 'at risk', without attending to riskier chronic conditions of intersecting, structural inequality.

CHRONIC CONDITIONS

I hope this last year has acted as a reminder to the mainstream that a life lived with conditions and restriction and fear is not fun. And that LGBT+ people might have been aware of this for quite a long time.

—Alice, 45, white, lesbian

On the anniversary of living with COVID under lockdown, I am angry. I am angry about the increasing resurgence of homophobia, biphobia and transphobia that our society has seen for a generation. I'm angry it has gotten so much worse under lockdown. I am angry that whilst the Government are trying to come to terms with this global pandemic, they've forgotten ... that AIDS was classed both an epidemic and a pandemic but our communities were abandoned and stigmatised.

—Clio, 35, white European/Mediterranean, bisexual, cis woman)

The United Nations report *COVID-19 and the Human Rights of LGBT People* highlights reduced and delayed access to medical services, discrimination, and stigmatisation.[12] This 'invisible baseline' featured in my conversation with LGBTQ+ organisations, activists, and interviewees. As one member of staff in a leading UK LGBTQ+ organisation put it:

> ... that's almost the expected cost of being queer, which particularly bites on working-class queers, queers of colour, disabled queers et cetera, that we're expected to kind of discount. And then we've had this kind of traumatic experience which everyone's living through, but we're particularly vulnerable in terms of isolation from chosen family and social networks and those sorts of thing, and particularly vulnerable to job losses.
> —Project worker, UK LGBT charity, interviewed 2021

Despite suggestions that we're 'all in it together' in the fight against the pandemic, we are not at the same 'baseline'. Conditions of poverty, poor health and housing, low income, and unemployment all unsurprisingly impact upon health, and with NHS waiting lists likely to remain long into the future, inequalities will increase. But measuring individual and even group experiences of the NHS as a discrete service can also work to separate out individual health entitlements from wider societal needs. Experiences of discrimination within the NHS are undoubtedly real and harmful.[13] Negative relationships with healthcare workers include experiences of prejudice, stigma, and microaggressions, and may lead LGBTQ+ people to be less likely to seek help, or even to test for COVID-19 symptoms.

Both working-class and middle-class interviewees expressed anxieties. However, more financially secure and privileged middle-class interviewees often expressed a confident entitlement to services which, even under crisis conditions, represented a realistic gauge of their experiences as entitled subjects (see Chapter 5). Clio, for example, continued to express a divide between NHS needs and LGBTQ+ needs, stating that 'many feel that healthcare providers don't have a good understanding of specific health needs of LGBT+ people'. This resonates with Jess (33, pakeha, lesbian, cis woman), who experienced delays in accessing NHS fertility treatment and opted to go private. The chronic conditions experienced by interviewees include the navigation of social and medical risk, as buffered by relative privilege and advantage, where working-class queers often don't fare well across the long-term.

Chronic conditions are just that – long-term and socially patterned rather than individual choices. And yet state-sanctioned solutions to the pandemic have been individualised and contained, understood as ones of self-sufficiency and household management: workers are to work from home and children are to be schooled at home. A dominant message has been 'stay safe, stay at home'. However, domestic safety is far from achievable for many queer people with unsafe homes, resulting in closeting, harassment, abuse, and homelessness.[14] The directive to 'be with your family' can still feel exclusive and unwanted and family is often not an easy site of belonging or return, where care can also be taken-for-granted, unrecognised, and coercive. Many people I spoke to told of being estranged from their families of origin, returning as 'guests', and making do by moving between 'scattered homes':

I've been pushed into the scattered homes of my elderly parents, my wife's mother, and finally my chosen siblings – mostly living as guest and caretaker in places I haven't lived since I grew into my identity as a queer, gender-non conforming adult. These experiences have been healing in some ways allowing me to make new kinds of relationships with blood family based on who I am now. In other ways these are really difficult and uncomfortable forcing me to be in areas that are much less welcoming to queer people and navigating healthcare structures not especially concerned about me or my family links. Honestly, I'm also really relieved that my wife and I were married in 2019, as this helpful and ridiculous legal protection has allowed us both to advocate for one another in healthcare contexts and to have some external legitimacy as a family. How often we've relied on this legal marriage this last year makes me angry and worried for other queer people whose relationships aren't so recognised by the state and the mainstream.

—EJ, 39, white, lesbian, cis woman

Queer intimacy often sits outside social expectations, traditional families, and relationships, with sexualities research long imbuing this with a disruptive and creative agency. Having 'families of friends' de-couples intimacy from 'biological kinship' in a movement towards chosen kin (yet policies, recognition, and supports often privilege family of origin over chosen relationships, and the choice to agentically foreground one's difference as a discerning, even responsible, or radically queer one, can be classed).[15] EJ recognised the power of being recognised as legally legitimate, thankful that she had married her wife pre-pandemic in 2019. She feels this both as 'ridiculous' and as 'relief', as echoed in Jasbir's (39, South Asian, lesbian, cis woman) question highlighting the gap between these state-sanctioned sentiments: 'Guidelines prioritise work, then families, but what happens for those of us who find more comfort in chosen families than our direct blood relatives?'

Interviewees shared a sense of pressure in socially distancing and negotiating new conditions, including domestic arrangements and intimacy. The instruction to 'stay at home' has felt alienating for many groups, and for many of those living in alternative family arrangements, such as partners living apart together. The guidance to stay 'at home' imagined a national citizen within a locally bound place and with a local support system – consisting of a 'bubble' of domestic pods, parents, families, and partners. Although restrictions have included exemptions around caring responsibilities and so on, some interviewees expressed a degree of anxiety around whether their relationships and domestic arrangements, within and between households, local authorities, and national jurisdictions, would be questioned or validated. These concerns crossed multiple spheres, including leisure, healthcare and the workplace, and were often underscored by surprise and further questions – as well as a matter-of-factness ('So we had a pandemic wedding!'

[Heather, 37, lesbian, cis woman]). Many spoke about what relationships, intimacy, safe space, and visibility meant for LGBTQ+ people in times of 'government enforced monogamy', which extends backwards – and forwards – in thinking about the penalisation, medicalisation, and criminalisation of certain sexualities, alongside the persistent state-sanctioning of respectable, domestic, monogamous coupledom:

> ... government enforced monogamy with individuals who live in our own assigned zones – such a strange concept! Who knows what a possible reconnection will look like at the other side of this?!
>
> —Amy, 31, white, lesbian

Rules and regulations were mobilised to justify or enact hostilities, with one couple, who described themselves as an inter-racial queer, lesbian couple, being repeatedly asked in service and public encounters if they were 'one household'. Such questions would not likely be asked of white, heterosexually presenting couples, with the pandemic also becoming a time to regulate and insist on supposedly proper ways of being public, thereby restricting queer bodies in space. Such restriction represents a continuation of longstanding prejudice, where racialised and sexualised 'others' are not recognised as 'family', or indeed as part of public policies and presences. Such 'micro-aggressions', experienced here across axes of sexuality and race, persist despite legislative reforms such as the Equality Act 2010. Indeed, promised equalities reforms were seen to be sidelined and seemingly deferred to post-pandemic, post-crisis times. Many interviewees expressed fear as to how the pandemic would affect the progress of equality, diversity, and inclusion issues, and Jackie (58, lesbian, trans woman) looked forward '... to the resumption of progress on the GRA [Gender Recognition Act][16] in Scotland'. Both Jackie and Devon highlight policy action points – such as reform of the Gender Recognition Act – as those to be returned to and resolved:

> ... massive progress has been made but I hope the pandemic shows that we can do, and I would say should do, more to achieve

equality. Is this too much to ask? ... Please, once this is all said and done, return some focus to the massive issues of inequality that the pandemic has thrown up.

—Devon, 25, white, bisexual, non-binary

During the pandemic, rainbow images, posters, badges, and flags were widely displayed in support of NHS efforts, often standing for hope and happiness, and in-it-together sentiment. The hurt and mistrust expressed below by Clio and Sandra is easily recognisable. Clio objected to a public repurposing of the Pride rainbow flag, seemingly stripped of its past and present LGBTQ+ meanings. But it is equally important to ask if and how queer inclusion could surpass symbolic gestures, interrogating who is represented beyond the bands of colour: could support for the NHS, for example, queer the public imagination of this institution as constituted through the efforts of Jaslene as a key worker on a visa, with little recourse to complaint, entitlement or hurt?

The visibility of LGBT+ communities is unintentionally reduced further by the re-purposing of the rainbow flag for the NHS. That flag meant something. It was our symbol of hope first... It was a trusted indicator of safe welcoming spaces across the world, of a home away from home. The re-purposing of the flag is also problematic within a medical context.

—Clio, 35, European/Mediterranean, bisexual, cis woman

... I am always worried I come across as unsupportive of the NHS and key workers. This is, of course, not the case. I have been a key worker myself throughout the pandemic, and have friends and family working in the NHS. My concern is that now I ask myself a question whenever I see a rainbow symbol, or a rainbow flag: is this support of LGBTQ+ people or support of the NHS? ... I still find myself spotting a Rainbow flag and getting excited that it's a new queer café or bar, only to see it's some office showing their NHS support.

—Sandra, 28, white, lesbian, cis woman

These tensions represent the back and forward between queer struggles for access, visibility, and entitlement. But they also cause pause on who and what is imagined as entitled: whose displacement is foregrounded? Who is entitled to feel anger as others manage their words and voices to not be seen as angry, to not lose a (NHS) workplace, residency, or home? There cannot be an easy resolution or queer closure to claims as always sanctioned and (de)legitimised by the state. The NHS has long been charged with saving the British public – yet it exists as a fraught site perpetually bound to the reconstruction of gender, class and race. The under-resourcing of key welfare institutions and key workers is a more realistic gauge of state intentions. Jaslene's experience represents the contractions of work, care, and queer, of being a key worker but one outside of go-to rainbow politicisations or affirmations.

REASONABLE ADJUSTMENTS:
MUTUAL AID AND NON-STATE SUPPORT

You will need to ask for help if you require groceries, other shopping or medications. Alternatively, you can order by phone or online. The delivery instruction needs to state that items are to be left outside, or in the porch, or as appropriate for your home.
—Guidance on gov.uk website, 2020

LGBTQ+ communities and organisations have leveraged collective resources to respond to the COVID-19 pandemic, as with the HIV/AIDS pandemic. Resisting a narrative of victimhood, destruction, and risk, queer communities can be thought of as ever-responsive to crises, and as actively sustaining communities. Terms like 'circuit', 'scene', and 'pop-up' may be useful to describe formations and networks constructed by and for LGBTQ+ people in remaking community, including in times of crisis.[17] Queer communities often self-organise and disseminate information and resources, and have done so over a long-term. The innovations through the pandemic have been imagined as including:

(1) the power of mutual aid networks,
(2) the power of institutional anchors in placemaking efforts,

(3) urban change related to homesteading and population shifts,

(4) innovations in the architecture and interior design of physical spaces, and

(5) opportunities to enhance social connection through augmented virtual engagements.[18]

Asking 'What Is Mutual Aid?', Big Door Brigade define this as '... a form of political participation in which people take responsibility for caring for one another and changing political conditions ... by actually building new social relations that are more survivable'.[19] Stories of new change through DIY and Mutual Aid cultures often collide with another sense expressed by working-class queers, that they have, in effect, been practising exactly this, and before such practices became claimed as queer, as reflected in Alexia Arani's[20] statement that 'long before COVID-19, many TQPoC [trans and queer people of color] were redistributing wealth, sharing meals, offering rides, and opening up our homes, while struggling to gain the support we need in the face of rampant racialized, gendered violence and structural inequalities'. Potentially understood as forms of queer mutual aid[21] in their support structures, practices, and politics, various groups opened during the pandemic as not-for-profit, pay-what-you-can-down-to-zero venues that potentially allow people to enter whatever their circumstances. These venues build on anti-capitalist, not-for-pink-pound models, with other local queer businesses also recommitting to alternative practices, including implementation of 'pay it forward' prepaid schemes for books, food, and other provisions.[22]

I Zoomed with Lewis (29, white, pansexual, gender queer) at the height of the UK's second wave. This wave saw escalating COVID-19 rates and regional lockdowns as nation states within the UK also increasingly diverged. Lewis spoke about his own and friends' homelessness, of being rehoused, living in overcrowded accommodation, sofa surfing, and squatting. Our online interview was garbled, with us finishing one another's sentences and questions – interrupted too by our various background noises and diversions (children, partners, animals and so on). Lewis apologised multiple times for his poor Wi-Fi signal, as the sound cut in and out, reminding me of the digital divide beyond just having an internet connection. I'd anticipated using the auto-transcription function, but Zoom struggled and entirely failed in transcribing two fairly broad Scottish accents (as we also anticipated and fuelled one another's colloquialisms). 'Queer' was continually smoothed over as 'clear'. For me, this 'clarity' signalled another smoothing, or glossing, over, of classed words, accents, and ways of being more generally.

Lewis was active in queer community networks by necessity, moving beyond family of origin or simply 'staying at home'. Like other working-class queers, Lewis was cautious about the limitations, efforts, and labour involved in sharing over the long-term, and before the popularisation or showcasing of mutual aid as exceptional. Increased attention to what mutual aid is – and what it might do and undo as politicised and collective survival – is welcomed.[23] But the power and potential of such moves are (un)done by classed-racialised-gendered actors. While mutual aid models of care and provision queer traditional family and mainstream welfare services, there are resource implications when voluntary groups and individuals stand in for failed, reduced, or incomplete state support. Despite doubts, Lewis articulated an optimism in checking-in on neighbours and friends, and spoke of an upsurge in donations to the community hub where he works:

> My optimism lies maybe in that more peer-to-peer care of looking out for each other. Keep an eye on each other … just like 'Are you alright? … I will just bring you round some tins and stuff'. And sometimes that allows really wonderful support relationships … I'm hopeful that some of that can remain.
> —Lewis, 29, white, pansexual, gender queer

A difference existed between the ongoing practices of routinely 'slipping a tenner' to neighbours, and the increased, although still occasional, donations of others: in his community organisation, Lewis noticed increased domestic donations as people decluttered their homes, making way for working at home. Forms of long-term support exist in the everyday ('… when I didn't have money I'd be like, "can I come and eat at your house because I can't afford to eat?"'

[Daria, white Eastern European, 28, bisexual, cis woman]). But, par-adoxically, these everyday patterns may be less visible than one-off gestures or exceptions. Lewis and Laura both moved between the pandemic as a site of change, personally and politically, and as a site of stasis, as queer choices were deliberated and denied:

> The LGBT helpline has had so many coming out calls. And that's during the pandemic. We had folk, they were isolated, but we also had all these people who are suddenly like '... I'm done when I come out of this, like year long struggle, I'd rather be a more authentic self'.
> —Lewis, 29, white, pansexual, gender queer

> ... in this pandemic I have thought a lot about the questions 'is my lifespan counted if I'm not visible, not online with rainbow emojis in my profile description, not visible and counted if I don't assimilate in certain ways?' What does it mean to want to be seen and want to be quietly and invisibly contributing to my communities without all the noise? When is invisibility also complicity in silence and bias? How is quiet pride appreciated?
> —Laura, 36, white, lesbian, gender queer

The cancellation of annual Pride events across 2020–21 brought a sense of loss of physical and politicised connections. In remote areas the impact of the closure of queer venues seemed to stretch back from and into the long-term, where permanent and pop-up events had '... closed [their] doors for the foreseeable future ...' (Douglas, 46, white, gay, cis male). Some spoke about the oppor-tunity to revisit the meaning and organisation of Pride events as commercialised and increasingly expensive outlets. But others welcomed the chance for community (in)visibility, without all the noise, which included developing a sense of connection in everyday public spaces such as libraries and schools, as safe venues where LGBTQ+ life needed to be represented:

> Libraries are a solace for the LGBTQ+ community as well ... There is even a dedicated 'LGBTQ+' section in the [Glasgow] library ... A lot of vulnerable people visit libraries, including

members of the queer community, as libraries are often a safe space for them. The pandemic has stalled the opportunity for people to relish all the amenities of their local library.

—Erin, 27, white, queer, cis woman

Morag (64, white, lesbian, cis woman) celebrated the online LGBTI+Elders Dance Club and spin-off sessions organised by members, sharing resources such as computers and iPads, and information about how to use Zoom. Such sharing was not always straightforward or successful and had its limits, with service users often also becoming workers without wages rather than simply willing volunteers. The borders of communities are real and not everyone feels a sense of fitting into place, either face-to-face or online.

Returning to Jaslene, queer spaces are also sites of normative expectations and exclusions. Her queer participation is often rendered precarious, where the LGBTQ+ places she participates in might also be somewhat off the queer map (for example, the gay choir, the queer walking group, and the lesbian football team). In attending, Jaslene may be understood as multiply 'coming out' and claiming visibility. Yet her presence is repeatedly troubled in getting inside – and by those on the inside. Despite the fluid nature of the walking group as 'turn up and join in', Jaslene, on doing exactly that, was asked if she was lost and whether she had properly understood the nature of the group ('… they were actually wondering whether I was just lost and joined them by mistake. I was like "Er, no!" [laughs]'). Effectively, this is a door policy, but not one of innocent safeguards: there are firm, clear, and repeated messages about who gets to belong and whose presence is always viewed with suspicion, hostility, or even 'host' friendliness. While Jaslene continues to attend the group and is now accepted, her attendance was conditional – on recognising and being recognised – in a way that it wouldn't be for white middle-class queers. Jaslene's queer departures and returns across different cultures, languages, and scenes is a queer sociality which implicates herself, and her family at a distance, whilst also evidencing the distance between and beyond queer community, including querying limited or extended, celebratory or reciprocal, 'mutual aid'.

CONCLUSIONS: BREAKING THE CIRCUIT

As post-pandemic life is grappled with, the queer left needs to struggle against (a return to) normal. Families are urged to step up and to be there for their 'nearest and dearest', where proximity becomes aligned with affective and material attachments. In contrast, others are expelled from national cares and connections: this is witnessed in the hoarding of vaccines and supplies, capitalist copyrighting, and heightened nationalism, even as UK supermarkets' basic supplies diminish, and Brexit makes the UK poorer. Arundhati Roy named the pandemic as a portal, taking us towards what is out of view or obscured. Yet the continuous failure of the state is repeated across crisis contexts: here the pandemic doesn't so much appear as a portal taking us into other futures but more as a vortex, or a trap. In supposed post-pandemic times, we are still in crisis. Things have been re-learned and achieved through the pandemic, including creative queer community responses, the lived reality of alternative family formations as 'families of choice', online Pride events, and Mutual Aid schemes. But ad-hoc emergency provisions come with questions around access and sustainability: what work will be recognised or undercut, reciprocated or appropriated, in these queer moments and as communities and individuals deploy DIY, and 'pay it forward'?

When LGBTQ+ people still often feel uncared for, at the back of the queue, and uneasy about performative rainbow flag support for the NHS, how can such unease be situated alongside Jaslene's experience as a migrant key-queer worker who becomes a 'space invader', including in queer communities?[24] Inequalities remain structured patterns embedded within existing systems, rather than exceptional or individual instances, or counts, of 'hate crimes'. For the queer-feminist researcher being trolled on social media (as in the opening extract) there are other enduring digital divides. I think about ageing populations in rural communities and the DIY efforts of equipping LGBTQ+ elders to be online. I think about Jaslene's video calls back home and her wish that her dog would face the screen.

In breaking the circuit – referred to as a way of intervening in escalating COVID-19 rates, but with a wider resonance for continued health and social inequalities – I think about lived experience, categories, and counts as (not) mattering in everyday and emergency times. Jaslene's response to my call for participants highlights (un)certainties around 'queer' and 'class'; she seeks confirmation that I'm interested in her classed experiences as not fitting-into the go-to story of class in the UK. Naming the whiteness of queer-class presences and projects becomes one response to Jaslene's questioning. Despite Jaslene's sense that our interview isn't 'going to hurt', often these things – purchase and pride in the categories of 'working-class' and 'queers' or a mis-fit and disconnection from these – do indeed hurt. These hurts are active and alive, negotiated too in fieldwork contexts, and made apparent when a working-class woman, earning a relatively low income, from a poor background in the Philippines highlights her distance from British ideas of class, community, and culture.

The COVID-19 pandemic has shown just how wrong the Brexiteers' message of protecting the NHS was. The disruption caused by Brexit exceeds the NHS and includes increased financialisation of citizenship entitlements including the right to remain, increasing hostility towards asylum seekers, renewed vulnerability of families surpassing national, nuclear containment, and a heightened sense among rural and marginalised communities of their peripheral, once EU-buffered, status. Unsurprisingly, these risks are unevenly navigated and intersect class, gender, and racialised inequalities. Chapter 4, 'Queer Provincialisms in (Post-)Brexit Britain', considers working-class queer experience in post-Brexit times and the making and breaking of 'Rainbow Europe'.

4

Queer Provincialisms in (Post-)Brexit Britain

... five years ago I would've called myself British, because I was against Scottish independence ... I was always ardently British. I would always say Scottish UK but I would always say 'I'm from Britain, I'm Great British', and that was my right. Scotland is more progressive than England and the UK as a whole ... I have been slowly pulled more towards 'I'm Scottish, not British', and I still couldn't honestly answer you whether I'd vote 'yes' or 'no' [to independence] if I got the chance again. But I'm certainly now Scottish not British, and that is because I'd rather be European than be British ...

—Lachlan, 24, white, gay, cis man

... if someone LGBT lived in Scotland from the beginning of his life they can see some problems with LGBT, but I lived in a country where there's oppression. So when I came here I found all the equalities and all the freedom. There are some problems. But I see that the government's still working on it. But in Morocco the government, it's still oppressing for LGBT communities and society is against it.

—Farj, 26, mixed-race, bisexual, trans person

The Brexit process has instigated significant transformation to the UK, to constituent countries, and to devolved relationships with Westminster. There may be signs of post-Brexit hope in queer reconstitutions within and across the borders of nation state(s), as challenges to state-centrism. State transformation matters to queers, as both Lachlan and Farj demonstrate. These matters take shape locally, nationally, and globally. Queer space might constitute a provincial move away from *the place* to be, generally scaled to the Global North as a US-centric measure.[1] Forms of provincialism enacted in 'wee places' might productively position against big nationalism. This extends to methodological nationalism, which assumes a fixed state rather than sites, subjects, and borders in flux. Scotland – out of sync with the wider UK in voting against Brexit – moves and extends towards 'Rainbow Europe' while contracting and distancing from Britain (and England specifically). In (post-)Brexit Britain 'queer provincialisms' are navigated in claims of and against (non)citizens. But 'Europeanising queer' for mobile 'world citizens' often acts to simply replace US-centrism with Euro-centrism, and heightens a binary between 'leading' and 'other' states.[2]

Nation states are differentiated as guarantors and protectors of LGBTQ+ rights, and homonationalism extends into small-spaces. The 'small space' I invoke here is Scotland as a devolved nation and constituent part of the UK. I do so as Scotland claims to be a different kind of nation, casting citizenship as civic, rather than ethnic, and as closer to Europe in its pro-remain outcome than it is to England/Britain. This transitional moment – between a failed state represented by the UK Westminster Government and a different state which the Scottish Government is often seen to embody – allows for an interrogation of nation states. There is queer potential in these transitions: some queers can enact their social and legal entitlements as full citizens, and the impact of Brexit has been limited to, for example, frustrations around potential travel delays or longer-term relocation retirement plans. There are important differences in the experience of mobility as intersecting inequalities are mapped onto new-old bordering practices, regimes, and institutions. Lachlan, for example, has the choice to move between Scottish-British identity categories, as politicised preferences, while others simply cannot choose (as seen in Chapter 3, where Jaslene wondered if she is, or ever will be, 'British enough'). Lachlan suggested an arrival at Scottishness as another kind of state, claim, and identity, notably as a sign of or signal towards being 'more European than British'.

Like Lachlan, some interviewees felt that space would be made in 'Rainbow Europe' to include the Saltire Flag, even as a 'leading light'.[3] Here Scotland takes up more space as a better place. While Lachlan refuses recognition, as 'not British', he does so as a British passport holder, whereas for Farj, Britishness was aspirant as well as ambivalent, bound up in a migrating middle-class status not easily capitalised upon in the context of a new country.[4] Claims about Scottish difference gloss over interviewees' lived experiences, wherein accounts of racism highlight the whiteness already at the centre of (homo)nationalist agendas, ever enacted in Scottish-British-European nation states. Racism, sexism, homophobia, and transphobia were specifically mentioned as enduring realities curtailing a sense of state transformation, including an imagining of civic or queer citizenship. Farj's case – outlined in this chapter in some detail – challenges an additive or static view of inequality and identity.

The (post-)Brexit period stretches backwards from the 23 June 2016 referendum and forwards beyond the 31 January 2020 exit, as the regressive–progressive potential of states exceeds the Brexit timeline.[5] In taking part in research during the period 2018–21, interviewees expressed a sense of pessimism and optimism, as well as a sense of stasis. I interviewed queer workers, residents, and parents, as well as those without employment, those unable to gain work, those with pending asylum claims, and those with families and communities in and beyond the new EU–UK borders. Some interviewees expressed a generalised nervousness around (post-)Brexit Britain, fearing a potential lack of recourse to leading progressive 'Rainbow Europe' equality law. However, less privileged participants had never felt included or protected by those same laws. Highlighting intersecting inequalities in the (post-)Brexit context means being sceptical about the descriptive listing of 'protected characteristics', and equalities legislation more generally. Such scepticism and uncertainty becomes a problem with respect to empirical measures and categories, including the ones adopted in, and accountable to, EU funding programmes.

PROJECT-ING WHITENESS: WORKING WITH (WHITE) EUROPE

… They think people in working-class council estates are Brexit crazy unionists, racist, homophobic, there's no place for us there,

there's no LGBTQ there. Which is just a lie, which is just not true.

—Dan, 36, white, gay, cis man

'Citizenship' in and across Europe was one of the main conceptual framings of the CILIA project[6] on intersectional lifecourse inequalities. In comparing distinctive nation states, the intention was to think about the stories and experiences of progress, and the ways in which nations, communities, and individuals claimed citizenship or were rendered un-entitled to it. The point wasn't just to produce a simplistic count of good/bad nations or to plot a linear path which moved queers from the 'other' category to a full social and political count. In moving from being EU citizens to no longer being so, even if they felt and expressed themselves as still 'European', interviewees in Scotland and England highlighted both the promise of and threat to citizenship and to 'Rainbow Europe'. EU participants often found themselves entangled in the bureaucracy of re-navigating citizenship rights, including welfare, employment, and residency. Within the research, Scotland was often collapsed into England, as England was conflated with Britain. Issuing objective correctives, also imbued with subjective affects, I too cast Scotland as not just a 'wee place' and as 'big enough'. I too navigate the questions of inter-nationalisms and provincialisms scaled to questions of who and what counts in the (post-)Brexit moment. As Dan's opening quote to this section implies, much can be at stake in the reduction of people and place, as council estates became represented as pro-Brexit concentrations, and the problem of Brexit became located as a problem of the white working-classes. As Dan's indignation suggests, this often was, and is, simply not true, misreading working-classes as homogeneously white and disguising the reality of more powerful middle-class Brexit voters.[7]

Research itself actively constitutes different categories and counts, summarised, represented, or still out of reach. Queer research(ers) involved in accessing 'hard to reach' groups will likely bump up against institutional ethics committees, where sexuality and other 'protected characteristics' become 'sensitive' topics: research is slowed down in these institutional processes even as institutional processes proclaim 'diversity!' has arrived.[8] Certain categories are rendered neutral – middle-class, cisgender, hetero-sexual, white, able-bodied – thereby becoming unproblematic on the demographic sheet; easy to tick-off, business as usual. Recognising some of these supposedly objective processes and categories as barriers in themselves, I started the CILIA project with the question of 'who to reach?' as a familiar repetition. LGBTQ+ groups and individuals are under-researched, with sexuality and gender being represented for the first time in the 2021/2022 Census.[9] And yet sexuality and gender are also over-researched as categories 'at risk' or as 'bad data' (Chapter 2). This binary of absence and excess is rendered more complex when considering the social and political motivations of participants, and attempts to (un)do queer data.

In researching queer communities I've used and omitted class terms on project information and in recruitment processes, finding that flyers – when unmarked as recruiting from LGBTQ+ populations generally – typically recruit white, middle-class, and gay cis men first. Aware of this, I decided to hold back in recruiting, to allow others time and space to come forward, and in particular to actively recruit across working-class and minoritised ethnic groups. I used a screening survey to balance those who'd rushed forward as eager LGBTQ+ citizens and those who held back. Gauging reasons for participating can also be an important factor to balance – with lots of enthusiasm amongst certain groups ('As an LGBTQ+ person ...') sitting alongside a responsibility, reluctance and ambivalence. Still, most CILIA participants (54 out of 60) were of white ethnic backgrounds, including participants from Scotland and the rest of the UK, Western, Central and Eastern Europe, the USA, Canada, and New Zealand. Six participants were Black, South Asian, South East Asian, and of Mixed ethnic backgrounds, including participants from Scotland, the rest of the UK, and Morocco. This lack of ethnic diversity is a project failure, but a failure that has a history as an embedded disciplinary practice so rooted that queer research projects may first be recognised as white projects, also imagining and projecting whiteness onto queer populations. This necessitates thinking outside the rainbow, and outside the normative markers even within queer populations, with whiteness constructed as central to LGBTQ+ identities.[10]

Most participants described themselves as Scottish or as being from Scotland: years spent in Scotland impacted upon a sense of and claim to 'being Scottish' when not 'born in Scotland'. For some, dual citizenship meant a material hyphenation of 'British-Scottish-and [...]'. In constructing a recruitment survey, I paused on the 'list of ethnic groups' in official surveys, including in expanded categories of whiteness.[11]

White
- English, Welsh, Scottish, Northern Irish or British
- Irish
- Gypsy or Irish Traveller
- Any other White background

Whiteness as a category may be neutralised in the seemingly benign list of tick-boxes from which to select – while the dominant effect of whiteness prevails. In responding to the categories used by the 2011 Census, the 'awkward etc.' box of 'Other, please state' was used. White participants used varied descriptors, to include, for example, 'White Scottish, Dutch, French-Canadian', 'Eastern European, Scottish', 'White European/Mediterranean'.

Participants of colour also modified and inserted Scottish descriptors (for example 'Scottish South Asian', 'Mixed Scottish'). British and Scottish national identity is racialised as white and the limited participation of people of colour is not just a result of category failures, such as in the 2011 Census list of ethnic groups, but of cultural exclusion, misrecognition, and racism, as Jaslene's case showed (see Chapter 3).

The project established a user group, composed of invested and experienced LGBTQ+ groups and individuals from across the private and public sectors. Often bringing the 'outside' in, and having non-academics present in academic forums, is seen as inclusive, and even as evidence of Equality, Diversity, and Inclusion (EDI) practices. Yet not everyone is equal and present at the table (see Chapter 2): one mainstream charitable organisation didn't know if they had any LGBTQ+ 'clients', and other organisations, whose focus and funding were primarily around race and religion, echoed this uncertainty. Uncertainties and inequalities abound in EDI spaces, with young people and people with disabilities also underrepresented in the user group – presence and participation can mean going around rather than beyond the table. Disclosures can become discrete, as redirections back to what and who *we did get*, to diversity across, for example, age-range, disability, sexuality, and gender identification.

Disclosures can happen without whiteness being disclosed: in talking about the lack of people of colour in the sample, the user group and its (non-)academic members (including myself) explained and excused, framing Scotland as 'not very diverse', as 96 per cent white. But a lack of ethnic diversity cannot be excused because of a supposedly low percentage 'ethnic population', just as queer researchers would not likely be content with a simplistic LGBTQ+ count. The Office for National Statistics estimated that 1.4 million people aged 16+ (2.7 per cent of the UK population) identified as lesbian, gay, or bisexual (LGB) in 2019. Between 2018 and 2019, there was an increase in those who stated 'Don't know' or refused to answer, from 2.5 per cent to 3.0 per cent (1.6 million).[12] Likely, queer researchers, groups, and individuals would want to challenge this low percentage count as then not amounting to enough, or as not mattering. In describing herself, Jess uses 'pakeha' as a Māori-language term for white New Zealanders primarily of European descent – although the term and usage is not without controversy.[13] Jess repeats the common-sense view of whiteness as just how-it-is, making 'quite white' difficult to refute:

And then coming to Scotland that was quite interesting because Scotland's quite white, and so I maybe don't see as much of what goes on as I had a glimpse into like race and gender relations in New Zealand. I haven't seen as much of it here because I think Scotland's ninety-seven per cent white.
—Jess, 33, pakeha, lesbian, cis woman

The CILIA sample was diverse in terms of sexual and gender identifications: respondents variously described themselves as lesbian, gay, bisexual, pansexual, queer, and asexual. Around a third of participants described themselves as trans, non-binary, intersex, genderqueer, or gender diverse; while the assumption might be that two thirds were cisgender, not all remaining respondents self-selected or applied this descriptor. This is suggestive of potential hesitancy around the category of 'cis', which may reflect its typically neutral or unmarked status, as with whiteness, middle-classness, or heterosexuality. Yet it may also reflect a deeper ambiguity too – a pause and uncertainty on behalf of interviewees – as well as assumptions from researchers that there is nothing to explore or unpack around cisgender as a category or lived experience.[14] Lesbian, gay, and bisexual interviewees did express varied experiences of inhabiting gender and sexuality queerly, of questioning normative assumptions of gender essentialism, of not inhabiting 'proper' femininity and masculinity, and many had been misgendered.[15] This is not to conflate these expressions and experiences into trans and non-binary experiences – particularly in the context of increased transphobia – but rather to continue to queer sexual-gender categories (see Chapter 6 for a discussion of 'lesbian' as a queer anachronism).

The screening survey asked questions about residency and local authority area, employment, education, income, partner and parental status, and class identity. Roughly half of interviewees identified themselves as 'working-class' and half as 'middle-class', although there were resistances and uncertainties around naming in class terms from 'Don't know' responses to 'Middle-class (if class still exists)', and from 'First Generation Immigrant, working-class' to 'US lower middle-class, working-class ancestry'. Moreover, subjective identification of class didn't always correspond to income or education levels.[16] Middle-class respondents, in particular, often articulated a sense of disadvantage in educational, leisure, and employment realms, causing a 'downward mobility' of sorts, while these respondents often remained objectively middle-class. Despite a sense of social discrimination and educational discomfort, or employment disadvantage, often explained via LGBTQ+ status, middle-class respondents typically achieved in education and workplace settings in ways which aligned with, rather than departed from, middle-class associations. Interviewees were mostly university educated, having at least an undergraduate degree, and most were in full-time employment. Of the six participants who were not employed, four were women, including two identifying as trans, and two were men, including one identifying as trans; five of these participants reported disabilities or long-term health conditions, including depression and anxiety. Almost half of participants reported a long-term health condition, which may suggest a heightened awareness, politicisation, or acceptability of self-reporting: these figures also resonated with the higher-than-average levels of sickness and disability reported by LGBTQ+ populations generally.

Naming, coding, and categorising advantage and disadvantage in the context of queer lives can be difficult, where ideas of 'Rainbow Europe' act as homonationalist gloss, or as queer-metrics, which 'world citizens' move into as included. The quote from Dan (36, white, gay, cis man) that opened this section resituates everyday, provincial progress within, rather than outside of working-class communities, often assumed to be regressive as 'Brexit crazy unionists', with 'racist, homophobic' feelings. He does so as a named carer to his partner who has disabilities, living in an adapted council house on benefits, and supported by their rural community, refusing the go-to 'left behind' homogenised and racialised narrative projected onto white working-class communities. Dan does this without explicitly naming the whiteness implicit in shaping community, progress, and protection. Queers are exposed to and endlessly exhausted by the state, as implicated in and surpassing post-Brexit queer fears.

WORLD CITIZENS IN 'RAINBOW EUROPE'

The loss of EU membership brings different fears for different queers. The idea of a 'Rainbow Europe', as signalled in a raft of EU-led equality legislation, can be both comfort and cause for concern. While some lamented the loss of a protective 'Rainbow Europe', others had never felt included within its realm. The very imagining of a 'Rainbow Europe' involves pink-washing nation states, while displacing homo- and transphobia onto other classed and racialised places and people inside (the 'council estate') and outside of Europe. Muslims, migrants, and refugees are repeatedly depicted as stalling and draining the progressive liberal state and

'Rainbow Europe'. Jasbir K. Puar defines homonationalism as 'an analytical category deployed to understand and historicise how and why a nation's "gay-friendly" status has become desirable as a marker of progress, modernity and civilisation'.[17] Nation-making in the UK has long exceeded its own borders, and its colonial past remains present, including in imagining itself as a global leader, with rhetoric about gender and sexual equality deployed 'in the invention of a civilized, mature Europe and its irrational, perverse, barbaric Others'.[18]

In interview accounts a generalised sense of anxiety in losing the protective capacity of 'Rainbow Europe' was pitted against the UK's 'hostile environment' ('I think my biggest fear is that we'll start going backwards'—Heather, 37, white, gay, cis woman):

... it's the European Union that's given a lot of rights to the gay community and the people who are in charge of Brexit don't seem to be prioritising that. So I do worry what would happen. At the same time I also feel like the LGBT community is confident in their own voice now, that if, you know, whatever were to happen we would campaign to stop, you know, our rights from being taken away.

—Grace, 32, white, bisexual, cis woman

There were evident queer articulations of still remaining, being and feeling European, where turning to Europe in the face of hostile national policies and events could offer other identifications and possibilities. Yet these feelings and choices were not uncomplicated or unrelated to material realities – claims of, for, and by 'world citizens' became statements and sites of privilege, where the 'wee place' of the local is extended globally. More privileged interviewees spoke of their travel plans being curtailed, where they had, for example, looked to relocate post-retirement to continental Europe. Often this ended up recirculating a hierarchy of places to be LGBTQ+, with even positive notions of progression ending up in this same framing loop:

So it's great to see how things have changed over time and how gay marriage has sort of spread like an excellent virus around the world and gone to more countries than I ever imagined

...

My partner and I both have, her in particular, she has quite a global outreach in her career, so there's the possibility we'll live somewhere else next after Scotland, and certainly it being a gay-friendly place is like top of the agenda, especially with us hoping to have a family.

—Jess, 33, pakeha, lesbian, cis woman

One interviewee, Ian (44, white, gay, cis man), spoke of how his arthritis worsened due to the UK weather: 'So I have been looking at house prices and things and where I might go, and things like Brexit scare the life out of me because of access to Europe, it could disappear.' Others also expressed concerns about the availability of healthcare and spoke of the possibility of seeking out new markets as mobile citizens. Some were awkwardly charged with self-managing their own healthcare, as also a way to manage being and identity in the world. Quinn (23, white, gay, non-binary), for example, was anxious that Brexit could mean 'I won't be able to access like HRT [hormone replacement therapy]', producing a 'kind of constant fear'. Such anxiety was related to a series of articulated costs, consequences, and challenges of moving to another country – in this case North America, with a private health system – as compared with the challenges of remaining in Scotland. While Quinn does, on balance, have a degree of privilege in being able to move with their partner, who is a dual citizen, their desire is simply to find a 'pocket of safety', to continue to access HRT, and to lead a more liveable life.

Within the articulation of chosen mobilities, and constraints, of imagining futures 'here' and 'there', existed real and important questions of basic citizenship entitlements and rights. Astrid spoke of chaos and uncertainty as she considered whether she'd be able to stay in Scotland and if her son would be able to access free education:

... it's unclear whether I would have unemployment benefits or rights to housing, and all of that is not resolved. It's a total kind of black hole in terms of human rights even. So all of the securities that we were counting on as European citizens are kind of disappearing. My son is also German so I'm also worried for him, whether university will be free, his future working and all of that. He's spent the majority of his life in Scotland and if I leave and he stays here could I ever move back? Would I lose my right to live in Britain?

—Astrid, 44, white bi-/pansexual, cis woman

Clio was also actively navigating legal entitlements between countries and between different legalised versions of what, who, and where constitutes a relationship or a family. Clio had 'come out' five or six years before our interview and expressed a sense of progress and of 'standing on the shoulders of giants, right, and not letting the [LGBTQ+] flag down', yet felt that the 'fights start again'. As a dual British and Greek citizen, Clio was now actively pursuing a French passport as part of this fight:

When Brexit happened I was like 'What are we going to do? Because Greece won't recognise our marriage'. They will now, because basically the EU rapped them on the knuckle and said 'alright you don't have to do gay marriages, but you have to recognise marriages'. So, but at that time I was like 'I need to go and get my French passport so that should we need to leave you can come with me as my spouse', you know?

—Clio, 35, white European/Mediterranean, bisexual, cis woman

Interviewees sought to navigate (post-)Brexit realities, with the sense of 'Rainbow Europe' often rendered more complicated in comparing and contrasting across place. This became even more acute when faced with institutional, legal, and medical barriers, and a queer experience of these, as progressive and/or regressive forces ever navigated through race and class. These ever-present intersecting inequalities surpass a count of 'protected characteristics' for (some) 'world citizens', with Farj's account highlighting many of these tensions.

Farj

Farj moved to Scotland in 2018 as a 26-year-old middle-class, mixed-race, bisexual, trans person. They were helped by the Free Church of Scotland and, as an asylum seeker, they were not permitted to work and were living on a minimum income, while undertaking voluntary employment. Farj grew up in Morocco, and speaks Arabic, French, and English. Discussing their youth and schooling in Morocco, Farj described life as being very difficult for LGBTQ+ people, meaning 'years and years' of childhood traumas, which they had tried to 'just survive', experiencing depression and anxiety. In many ways mirroring go-to social stories about the location of homophobia and transphobia, Farj then attributed this to the specific Moroccan and Muslim culture they'd lived in, where LGBTQ+ life 'didn't exist'. From a middle-class background, Farj went to university in Morocco and France. While in France they converted to Christianity and established distance from the Muslim communities they'd previously been part of ('… I've been converted to Christianity in France, so I could feel safe from our communities, from Moroccan communities'). Farj described their conversion to Christianity as following a chosen, individualised path, free from 'culture' or 'tradition', as opposed to 'following like sheep', a disposition which they projected onto contemporary Pakistani communities in Scotland who '… live as communities …'.

Farj described how they couldn't 'find myself there', in France, deciding to move to Scotland. They expressed a sense of contentment in arriving in a 'safe place' where accessing legal support and healthcare was 'easy' ('… I've got my GP and she's very, very friendly … and especially when we talk about the trans process'). They were not 'out' to their broader 'church family' but were to the (white, Christian, Scottish) family they lived with. Scotland was described as the 'most friendly country for LGBT', attributed to a 'neutral culture', variously described as Christian and specifically not Islamic. At the time of their interview in 2019, they were seeking asylum in Scotland. In recounting their journey through legal processes, Farj spoke of not 'coming out', nor using, let alone embracing or identifying through, the categories of LGBTQ+, conscious of how people might judge them. Farj had to navigate fear and shame, later coming to understand this as a 'normal' part of claiming asylum, with an updated and official statement about their LGBTQ+ status then made to the Home Office via their lawyer.[19]

Farj invokes a racialised global hierarchy of LGBTQ+ liveability – yet it is one they are also judged by and implicated in rather than removed from. Their attribution of 'No problem here', in positioning Scotland as the best place to be LGBTQ+, didn't always measure up to relative comparisons.[20] Yet Farj seemed to have settled into a fit that was 'good enough', positively investing in a place and community which they could not afford to bad-mouth or spoil. Incidents of transphobia or homophobia were pushed to other people and other places ('I know that there is transphobic, LGBT-phobic persons, but I heard many stories in England, not in Scotland'). Hate crime was attributed to hateful others, to foreigners and outsiders, with 'the village' or 'somewhere' signalling an otherness, as uneducated or unsophisticated:[21]

> It can be from foreigners that they came from other countries, that they are anti-LGBT communities, but not for the local people … it's just words from someone who lived in a village or somewhere.

Farj's account – negotiated as someone often on the outside and navigating ways in – complicates the story of LGBTQ+ progression and its alignment with 'best countries' – even as this is also repeated. The story of 'Rainbow Europe' is already fractured in Farj's experience of movement, including via France, and where their arrival in Scotland may not be the end destination. Farj expressed a desire to live in the USA, specifically in San Francisco, where things would, they felt, be 'much better'. Significantly, their move was also seen as an opportunity to connect back to Morocco, albeit from a distance:

... I'm still working on it [asylum claim] and at the same time if things don't go well, because I have an opportunity for United States, and if I go to United States I will go directly to San Francisco, it's the best city there ... So I got an opportunity, it's Green Card lottery, the United States, they do it every year ... And if I get a lot of protection there in United States I will fight for the rights in Morocco, and even I can go to Morocco with safety.

In many ways Farj's account is understandably pragmatic, with Morocco, as their birthplace, lingering as a comparative backdrop. Local political protest around the insufficiencies of the UK state, manifested through Pride presences and placards, for example, are placed within this ever-present comparative context:

... I saw someone has a banner and he said the government doesn't care about trans people ... And when I compare it to Morocco it's, it's a big thing. Complaining about it, I found it, I don't find my place to complain about it. If I was in Morocco I would complain about everything there for LGBT rights, but here in Scotland as a trans person I get access to the healthcare, I get access to, I get appointment for the transition, medical transition. I know that in the education there can be some discriminations, but it's in the society not the government. And some services can be hard to change their laws. Here it can be the government that needs to do their job.

In such claims and contestations of governments (not) doing their job, the very purpose of the nation state comes into question. The Scotland which Farj arguably ambivalently settled into, while still awaiting settlement via their asylum claim, is a place which will judge and categorise them as a non-citizen. Navigating this, while telling of seeking another 'best place', perhaps highlights the impossibility of finding home or of ever fully being in place when deemed not from a place. Accounts such as Farj's illuminate who and what is at stake in re-bordering nations and citizens, even in the story of the good nation. Increasingly, queer theorists seek to erode the dominance of US-based queer thinking which, by omission, becomes in effect its own 'area based' (USA) study.[22] The local or provincial, particularly when situated in the Global South, is seen to counter or interrupt queer theory – and queer lived experience – as of and for the Global North. In many ways Farj's and others' movements and imaginings of themselves as world citizens empirically implicate and illuminate this binary. Farj's complicated appraisal of Scotland as the place to be, is queered too by ideas of 'Big Scotland' taking on 'Little Britain'.

QUEER IN A WEE PLACE:
FROM LITTLE BRITAIN TO BIG SCOTLAND?

I think Scotland's a leading light ... Why do we not want to connect across the world and use our knowledge of what we're doing in Scotland and spread the love a bit about what we're doing in Scotland?

—Ian, 44, white, gay, cis man

Contemporary (re)imaginings of Scotland as a different place stretch across centuries, animated in the present through devolution and independence debates. Reminiscent of Gloria Anzaldúa's (1990) 'border thinking', Sweta Rajan-Rankin (2017) argues that Brexit re-exposed national myths, leading to increased distinction and division between 'us' and 'them', as well as 'then' and 'now'.[23] Many interviewees spoke of the Brexit process as entangled with new and old feelings around Scottish independence, and some 'No' voters who wanted to remain part of the UK spoke of voting for independence in the future if that meant staying in Europe. For those who had already voted for Scottish independence, Brexit became an affirmation that Scotland should have left the UK and sought out other allegiances (even if this wasn't offered then or now).

Claims of difference, or Scottish exceptionalism, can function to gloss over inequalities, including shared legacies of and benefits from UK colonialism. The prevailing 'hostile environment' across constituent UK nations persists, with increased hate crimes reported across race, gender, sexuality, and disability.[24] Yet, despite evidence to the contrary, both Westminster and Holyrood Parliaments now make bold claims of being 'world leading' on LGBT inclusion. Claims appear in country counts of being the 'best place for LGBT rights', the 'friendliest gay city', or 'world leading' in LGBT+ inclusive education. Such border narratives are a fundamental part of the problem of states, as actively constituting a deeply racialised global hierarchy of (in)tolerance and (un)acceptable others and elsewheres.[25]

Scotland has been long mis-placed as *only* provincial, as small, regional, and rural, particularly via a Scotland–England comparative count of population sizes, big cities, and so on. It has come to embrace this comparison as a sign of difference, with the diminutive 'wee' of Scots arguably symbolising a linguistic, cultural, and broader socio-economic departure, from England specifically, and Britain more generally. The prevailing political context of Scotland also questions the purchase and potential of 'queer provincialisms' in post-Brexit Britain. Scotland is arguably dismissive of longstanding similarities in terms of racist, sexist, trans- and homophobic pasts and presents shared across constituent UK terrain, while also capitalising upon a sense of its own world-leading status. Within imaginings of Scotland as a subjugated place, exploited or underrepresented through Westminster rule, claims for Scottish independence re-emerge, especially around the flashpoints of Brexit, austerity, the COVID-19 pandemic, and the cost-of-living crisis. Speaking of the (pre-Brexit) 2014 independence referendum, Cat Boyd and Jenny Morrison, who were both involved in the Radical Independence Campaign, pitched independence as an opportunity for a radically different society, rather than more of the same:

> This is a case for radical change, which seeks to expose the current system and explain what 'better' would look like. We don't want to see a post-Yes Scottish society that's simply more of the same.[26]

Sally (56, white, lesbian) was originally from England, but had called Glasgow home for nearly 30 years, explaining that she was 'trying to get as many friends as possible to kind of move up here', contrasting the pessimism of Brexit with the optimism of Scotland as a 'pulse point' of change. This was reflected in other statements of Scottish difference as a 'leading light':

> I do think there are cultural differences that aren't expressed terribly well through Westminster. There are cultural nuances that I think in Scotland, in terms of LGBT rights I think we're a bit further forward than perhaps other parts of the UK, or we'd like to think we are.
>
> —Amy, 34, white, bisexual, cis woman

> Our problem always is that at the end of the day all major rules are made down in England, and I don't think England is quite as progressive as Scottish people tend to be. Scottish people always tend to be a bit more to the left and a bit more kind of open, politically at least.
>
> —Rose, 45, white, lesbian, cis woman

Within some interviewee accounts, a simple 'better than England' approach became the measure through which to recognise and celebrate Scottish difference, often stated as self-evident rather than something to explain or work towards. The positioning away from a 'toxic England', to quote one interviewee, may be part of a Scottish exceptionalism, which exempts itself from the weight of the (UK) 'past', while continued sexual nationalism re-magnifies the borders around states, citizens, and others:

> I think we're lucky in Scotland because I think it's better up here than it is in England. And it [Same Sex Marriage] kind of passed with no fanfare, everyone was like 'well obviously we're going to vote for it' … Whereas in England there was all these massive debates … So, you know, I kind of feel as if this is better than most places to stay. And I think it's been proven actually, it's better to stay in Scotland than anywhere else for LGBT rights.
>
> —Lorna, 38, white, lesbian, cis woman

> I think it's far and away better here than England. I think like England is a hellscape (laughs) and, yeah, just everything is worse there.
>
> —Lexi, 32, white, lesbian, trans woman

While my intentions are not to mis-place interviewees' investments in a nation that might be becoming 'for them', feelings of ambivalence and disappointment also circulate in these claims. Scottish 'difference' wasn't always straightforwardly articulated, and others felt let down by continued uncertainty, including the retraction of support and resources for LGBTQ+ equalities initiatives and policies in a supposed moment of Scottish difference. Lexi qualified her above statement with a warning not to take the 'foot off the gas', with Scottish progression marked by more conservative flashpoints but still comparing favourably:

> Scotland was, at one point, like right at the forefront of kind of moving, especially LGBT, equalities legislation forward, and then like took our foot off the gas ... I don't think this is like the best place in the world to be LGBT, but like I think it's pretty good. Definitely I would compare it favourably with the majority of the world, I guess.
>
> —Lexi, 32, white, lesbian, trans woman

Claims to difference were also viewed with suspicion, as a repeated policy gloss meaning that '... all forms of discrimination just evolve around legislation ...' (Alisha, 39, South Asian, lesbian). Alisha noted the stereotypes around Scotland and Scottishness, '... which has a very benign series of cuddly and cosy stereotypes associated with it', as bypassing some of the negative associations with Britain and/or England. National distinction in the idea that 'Scottish gays are better than any other' was similarly questioned by Dan:

> I don't believe in like, like 'Scottish gays are better than any other gays' and all that rubbish ... and I'd like our community to do so much more in, and challenge its own like internal homophobia, racism, transphobia, all this jazz.
>
> —Dan, 36, white, gay, cis man

Both Dan and Alisha's accounts expose the discrepancy between Scotland as a new civic nation, and its enduring ethnic nationalism, embodied and embedded in the histories and presences of homophobia, transphobia, and racism:

It's hard not to have a really deep cynicism about Scotland because of the volume of racism I experienced growing up and all these other things, like and the history of the SNP being a relatively right-wing party. I'm like, we're only, we're always just a few steps away from that history and that legacy ... I've said I'm Scottish as a way of distinguishing myself, or distancing myself, from what feels like a particularly toxic brand of politics operating in the country right now. But my passport and the rights I have to be in the country belong to this weird union. And I'm like, the larger and more diffuse the unit I can belong to the better, or more specific. Like I'd rather be European or Glaswegian (laughs). Like I either want to be super-specific or super-general. And I feel comfortable saying that I'm Glaswegian. I'm a product of its institutions. Or I want to be European, because it doesn't really mean anything. Whereas right now British really feels like it's a negative term. But I still find Scottish an unsatisfactory term, and as it becomes more political and less just a factual designation of something the less likely I am to associate with it.

—Alisha, 39, South Asian, lesbian

Alisha's account is multiple and intersecting, moving across times, yet by-passing the supposed 'arrived at' LGBT state as leading showcase, or 'white light'. Whiteness is fundamental to Britishness and Scottishness, and the incorporation of Black and Brown bodies has not significantly altered the white 'face of the nation' even as it has been obscured by 'the cloak of the "post-racial"'[27] or the rhetoric of the all-inclusive civic-state.

CONCLUSION: QUEER POSSIBILITIES IN THINKING BEYOND THE STATE

State transformation has different consequences for different queers as witnessed in the re-placing of nation states via the Brexit process as 'big', 'wee', 'provincial', or 'world leading'. Many interviewees' accounts echo queer assessment of exhausting and exhausted state processes, with some more subject to social and institutional regulation than others, including through persisting and pernicious asylum-seeking processes, as in Farj's case. Brexit has increased racism: Boris Johnson's 'Vote Leave' campaign was built on racist, xenophobic rhetoric that blamed immigrants for 'burdening Britain' and supposedly stretching educational, social, and healthcare systems. Such recent rhetoric and policy is in fact a long time in the making and the rhetoric of difference – as inclusive, civic, and specifically Scottish – does not necessarily step away from these historical presences. Farj's experiences – like others who are actively holding, pursuing, and/or lamenting citizenship access and entitlements – can be understood as ever-emergent from state-sanctioned racism, homophobia, and transphobia. As a provincial move away from homogenised Global North terrain, researchers can expose policy and methodological nationalisms, texturing 'Rainbow Europe' as *the place to be* while highlighting its unmarked whiteness. Lived experiences in provincial, local, everyday places often collide with and surpass the rhetorics of re-imagined states, which typically instrumentalise LGBTQ+ rights for the consolidation of nationalism. Queer-left agendas need to be concerned with the hopeful and pragmatic possibilities in queer reconstitutions within and across the borders of the nation state, in looking backwards and forwards. As a case, this was demonstrated in Farj's articulated hopes of relocating to the USA via Scotland so that they can look – and go – back to Morocco. But these re-orientations are represented in everyday 'provincial' as well as in 'exceptional' or even 'cosmopolitan' travels, as articulated by Dan in placing a working-class rural Scottish community at the centre of queer provincialisms. Chapter 5, 'Queers and Austerity', turns to the decade-long period following the global financial crisis of 2008 and highlights queer 'austerity scenes' as everyday crises preceding Brexit.

5

Queers and Austerity

... it's [same-sex marriage] creating a sort of two-tiered world where you are kind of jolly and out and no problems and equal to straight people and then the kind of slightly grotty ones who decide not to. You know, like an underclass, and I'm in that! (laughter). I'm in that underclass ... again!
—Katerina, 52, white, lesbian, interviewed 2008

I'm not going to blame being trans, I'm just going to blame the recession.
—Leigh, 35, white, straight, trans woman, interviewed 2009

I've been quite involved with the anti-austerity, anti-cuts stuff, done a lot of direct action when I've been well enough. I got arrested, that's not an experience I want to repeat ... I started doing creative protests, getting into shop windows of tax-dodging companies and posing as mannequins with messages. And obviously the shops hate it but the public really likes it. I love dressing up!
—Estelle, 25, white, queer, lesbian, interviewed 2013

In response to the global financial crisis of 2008 the UK government initiated wide-ranging austerity policies with large-scale public funding cuts, the effects of which continue to be felt and exacerbated through the Brexit and COVID-19 crises. The long austerity period saw an increase in zero-hours contracts, the freezing of child benefit, and other substantial changes enacted through the Welfare Reform Act 2012, including the replacement of Disability Living Allowance (DLA) with the Personal Independence Payment (PIP). The Bedroom Tax saw social housing tenants lose up to 25 per cent of their benefit if they had a 'spare' room. With these reforms came a heightened moral positioning of working-class groups as undeserving of benefits, lazy, and fraudulent, acting to justify the retreat of the state.[1] In official discourses, policies, and everyday representations, groups of people were seen as unworthy of a 'liveable life'.[2] Such state-sanctioned stigma became felt and normalised in everyday encounters and in popular representations, embedding and justifying inequality. With this came renewed legitimisation of the location of power and resources in the hands of the few, resourced by their own self-perpetuating networks and capitals, and congratulated for it.

Here, I think about queers and austerity across three intersecting scenes which weave in state policy and everyday inequality: queer urban presence and absence; claimed and contended family space; and colliding or reconciled queer-religious spaces. These sites have been multiply positioned and contested as marginal–mainstream, inside–outside, and radical–conservative, with such binaries re-circulating as intimate disruptions in austerity contexts, even as some LGBTQ+ citizens are invited in and acquisitively take up space. Different types of queer life persist through austerity, where forms of middle-classness make life more liveable for queers. Here, precarity is acknowledged as present in middle-class life, as, for example, a lack of recognition at the school gate, or as otherwise normative family credentials disrupted by queer existence. The long-term landscape of austerity is tied to normative expectations around gender and sexuality, with welfare displaced from the state onto families as a reasonable, responsible adjustment. Austerity policies call on people and places to be resilient, responsive, and regenerative, with middle-class queers better equipped to be recognised and further resourced in these calls, self-recognising as entitled, including as discerning consumers and proper parents located in the right kinds of scenes. These are intimate, interpersonal, and relational struggles, with classed distinctions and inequalities actively produced by queers: right and wrong 'choices' are apparent in the spatialisation of (parenting) privileges, and in the re-imagination of austerity as that which *others do* and *are*. Managing crisis is even evidenced as another success for middle-class families and individuals, and as distinct from working-class persistence, 'in the underclass ...... again!'

Queer scholars have used austerity and precarity in a variety of senses, including in probing whether queer theory is still queer, empirical, activist, or everyday.[3] For working-class queers, especially those who are trans, disabled, and/or people of colour, fundamental questions delimit the possibilities of existence and persistence, including through benefit retraction and unemployment. Both Leigh and Katerina signalled the uneven experience of austerity and precarity in the above excerpts; while Leigh vocally redirects blame towards structural inequality and the global recession, her statement comes as a deflection against being set up as a figure of blame and shame, frequently represented as part of an 'underclass' in the moral and material economy of UK austerity. In exploring the sexual and intimate life of austerity, this chapter asks 'what makes life more liveable for queers?' Recognising pragmatism, persistence, and survival is also located in an intersectional frame which understands racialised and classed communities and actors as *having* to get by.

The extension of citizenship rights to *some* LGBTQ+ citizens aligns with the vision of good, responsible, well-managed lives, then mobilised as a stigmatising and contrasting repertoire against 'undesirable others' and ultimately furthering neoliberal austerity. Working-class queers often have their own forms of getting-by, even as they remain outside of the cultural and social legibility enabling middle-class queers to be visible: non-state supports exist in different scenes, including in faith structures, which often absorb those left-behind, even as religion is set up as a clashing force from which the state must protect queers. In looking for non-state solutions to the exhausting and exhausted state, these long-term experiences highlight how cumulative austerity and precarity is lived with, thus departing from framing austerity policy as a response to exceptional crisis.[4] Supposedly unprecedented crisis times are enduring and persistently recognisable as decades of austerity, as areas of chronic deprivation, as a promise of 'social levelling' which never arrives. Austerity is yet another articulation of the long-term retrenchment of the UK welfare state, challenged through a long history of queer-feminist, anti-poverty, anti-racist, and disability activism. There are many examples of 'austerity scenes', and here I focus on just three to locate queers and austerity: in the provincial North, stretched and shattered by the pink promise of 'Gay as Now'; in articulations of lesbian and gay parenting, seemingly rendered visible and acceptable as a result of equality legislation; and in the queer case of religiosity, often neglected as a queer-class scene. These scenes sit together as possible sites of solidarity and as still queer(ed) and class(ed) practices of care, inclusion, kinship, and community.[5]

ACADEMIA, OUTREACH, AND AUSTERITY, OR BECOMING MIDDLE-CLASS?

... there was people from [LGBT health and well-being service] and they were saying 'we do outreach to that area'. And even that word outreach, so like the metropolitan gays are coming out and patting us on the head?

—Gavin, 50, white, gay man

In working with community groups over the longer-term, I've arguably been complicit in the kind of patronising, do-gooding 'outreach' that Gavin details. I've had many discussions about what community and commercial organisations could be, who to preferably, reliably, or ethically partner with, where to host annual mainstreamed or alternative Pride events, and where to avoid. I've been warned against placing the free Pink Paper in certain venues, as queer presences have moved from the corners of community rooms, to shop fronts, to entirely online. I've taken part in LGBTQ+ rainbow parenting events, in pride in the park days, in queer worship, as deliberately different from go-to venues and representations of queer life. I've had voluntary roles within the LGBTQ+ sector and have been part of sustaining precarious groups through crisis times, as premises and funding have been lost. I've done this in, through, and as (at times maybe even instead of) my academic work. I continued with this work before and during a period where this became measurable as 'impact', as the university extended its outreach and dialoguing with 'real life'. This work has been both strategically instrumentalised and rendered suddenly invisible, colliding with long-term queer-feminist effort done, practised, and even failed, over careers, cares, and connections.[6] In these efforts, communities become the bad data which can be acted on (Chapter 2), nudged forward, and even transformed as others' 'outreach'. Queer-feminist practices lead me to trouble whose 'real life' we are mobilising, in and as outreach, and in the austerity regimes that we buffer and sustain: is there a queer way to reach out, or does that gesture always signal a redirection towards middle-classness? The period of UK austerity overlapped with my own 'coming of age' in academia, as I gained my first permanent full-time academic position in 2005. The 'early career researcher' category hadn't been named as something to resource or politicise. My educational experiences meant that I didn't feel automatically entitled to be in university, or to have a career (see Chapter 3). While increasingly subject to problematic outreach initiatives as an awkward widening participation invite into the university – anticipating self-change from invitees – in many ways working-class life *does* prepare working-class academics for later hardships. Meritocracy, entitlements, and pragmatism constituted early career introductions to academia – then as now – and I've always balanced a sense of comparison with middle-class peers. As the 2008 financial crisis hit, I continued to pay off my student debt and I continued to travel to care for my elderly grandparents. In practice, flexible or agile working hadn't extended beyond immediately recognisable nuclear families, despite the Equality Act 2010. I travelled, cared, and managed a career across the North–South divide; I argued with the NHS about end-of-life care, and was seen as un-caring in my single status; I invoked 'family' and 'community' and felt the promise, weight, and failure of these. These contradictions represent the intimate disruptions fuelled by austerity politics and navigated through personal-professional-political contexts.

As a queer-feminist researcher I have critiqued and existed within the elitist structures that celebrate individual success (for white, cis-het, middle-class men). In gaining a permanent academic position, I was often told that I'd become middle-class, the potential of outreach fulfilled with the promised arrival. Yet my research outed my distance from that state, and I felt the weight of my book *Working-Class Lesbian Life* (2007) as use, return, promise, politics. I felt the lack and lag between anticipated earnings and entitlements (and embodied dispositions) in being or becoming academic. In many ways the positive aspects of career and geographical mobility accrued, now arguably necessary for any (academic) career. I relocated with long-term material attachments to the places and people I'd moved with and through. Yet I did so in a political climate which emphasised individual responsibility and entrepreneurial investment: the university (and the university career) became a site of neoliberal practice, marketisation, and 'selling out'.[7] This caused pause on what feminist-queer classrooms were becoming, as well as a suspicion about supposedly good-old-university-days (when people like me wouldn't have got in). In accessing university, experiencing career mobility, and occupying senior management positions, I've fielded questions about my authenticity or otherwise as sharp reminders of lag and lack; of being the unexpected arrival within middle-class realms, even when yielding career credentials, and conversely of being late to the table. I've arrived at the table as it's been upturned – with 'death of class debates' countered by 'big data' on class, extended by analysis on classed discourses, cultures, and representations.[8] I arrived as 'intersectionality' cycled in and out of academic and popular currency as feminist classrooms of the 1990s and 2000s were institutionally cut, and as queer moved from being anti-identitarian back to an identity count of LGBTQ+ people.[9] My theoretical, conceptual, and geographical references – as well as my political and personal ones – have been (re)mapped in these moments, and I've lost and found my ways in and out of the communities that I've been part of, including different metropolitan – or provincial – ones. In 2010 I moved from the northern province of Newcastle to *the big city*, as I took up a scholarship at Rutgers, living in view of the New York skyline. On return to the UK in 2011 I relocated from Newcastle to London. Like other English cities at the time, London was experiencing riots across the city sparked by the fatal police shooting of Mark Duggan, a 29-year-old Black man from Tottenham, North London. Then London Mayor Boris Johnson and Prime Minister David Cameron dismissed the idea that the riots were related to government cuts, the effects of growing levels of poverty, or racial tensions, claiming these to be the outcome of criminality, greed, and opportunism – a 'twisted moral code'. So set in an embedded programme of state-sanctioned blaming and shaming, fuelling hate against those facing the full brunt of social inequalities. Members of the Scottish Parliament frequently voted to the left of their Westminster counterparts on austerity measures, with Scottish difference a key claim of the 2014 independence referendum (see Chapter 4): I lived in London in 2014 and, as a non-resident, wasn't entitled to vote in the referendum, but was sceptical about both Scottish and English claims around (anti-)austerity. My sense of outreach and what is left out-of-reach in-between states, sites, and communities is a queer one, echoed by the working-class queers in this chapter.

AUSTERITY SCENES

Scene 1: Bright lights, big city

> ... someone went past and tripped over my wheelchair and said, 'Who left the pram in here?' I get more hassle on the gay scene for disability issues than I get for being gay in the straight world, which was a surprise when I became a disabled person ... And out of the two discrimination issues I experience the disability one by far, I come across on an almost daily basis.
> —Fred, 45, white, gay man

UK LGBT Politics Crash Course: What Austerity and the Far Right Mean for Queers[10] lists a range of effects, including homelessness and unemployment, starkly colliding with the imagined protections of the UK Equality Act 2010. Implemented as austerity measures, LGBTQ+ support services have faced devastating cuts, including the refusal of NHS England to fund HIV prevention drugs in 2016.[11] Structural conditions have long shaped the viability and even legality of LGBTQ+ services and premises, as sites of protection, commerce, and mainstreaming. Pre-recession the mainstreaming of commercialised scene spaces became a heightened part of urban rebranding. The interpellation of particular queer subjects as *consuming* subjects has had some positive or seductive effects, producing a sense of validation and legitimation.[12] But in the 'cosmopolitanisation' of cityscapes class is made and done, and with this has come an abjection of 'those more distanced from and threatening to the mainstream, such as the poor, ethnic/racial/ sexual minorities, drag queens, and butch lesbians'.[13] Austerity scenes extend beyond the physicality of spaces, ever-shaping entry points, and move into a moral economy which generates its own normative presences and absences, felt on an 'almost daily' basis by interviewees, including Fred, as expressed above. Not long after meeting Fred, the Equality Act 2010 was enshrined in UK law, legislating for a series of protected characteristics, including disability and parental status. Fred, and other working-class queers, were caught up in these policy promises and retractions, where they were rarely on time or in place to be 'Gay as Now'.

Fred's experience of Newcastle's changing scene space could not be separated from his wider socio-economic circumstances as someone impacted by the ending of Disability Living Allowance (DLA). As a 45-year-old disabled gay man and wheelchair user, Fred named the increasing cutting-back of services and supports as eroding his access to care, leisure, and compassion, fuelling a hostile disablist sentiment, including in LGBTQ+ scene spaces. At the time of the interview Fred wasn't in work: his benefits had been subject to monitoring and reduced and he was anxious about getting by. I'd arranged to meet Fred in my workplace, checking the accessibility of the space – reading the official institutional policy on this as sufficient: 'lift access is available'. On meeting, it soon became obvious that the accessible building was in fact inaccessible. Fred tried to get into the building. I tried to help. Fred tried to make me feel better in my embarrassment and frustration, as common feelings felt and deflected by Fred as part of his daily access. Fred's story surpasses the story of the lift, as a question of long-term inaccessibility, sharply felt in the context of austerity, where Fred's access to a personal carer was also under review (then ending and making him physically and financially dependent on his partner). Reactions to and discrimination against Fred as a disabled person constituted a profound barrier to entry, even as a literal locking down and out (and well before the pandemic lockdown). His experiences come up against others interviewed, such as Sabina (26, white, lesbian) who, although complaining of profound misogyny in scene spaces, stated, 'I suppose they're accessible, you can just walk right into them.' In thinking who and what mis-fits scene space, families and parents have been named as obvious absences, and Janice (44, white, lesbian) was vocal in her desire for accessible 'family-friendly' queer spaces. While intended as an inclusive gesture, Janice named 'prams and wheelchairs' in the same sweeping sentence, as a de-sexualised collapse felt by Fred in being pushed out of the scene.

Engaging with queer lives as differentiated means situating local specificities. In 2008 I spent time with an LGBTQ+ group in Teesside, an area subject to long-term disinvestment, with declining life expectancy rates attributed to austerity policies. I witnessed the awkward investment and direct disinvestment in the LGBTQ+ group. In attending, I was typically met with an abundance of sexual health literature, posters, advice lines, and so on. Information on sexual health 'risk' was an enduring presence in – and has often been a funding stream for – community venues (before and through austerity periods and into the COVID-19 pandemic period). 'At risk' messages were often overwhelming, indicated in wall-size posters, in ever-present jars of condoms and needle-exchange depositories. 'Service users' seemed to feel a similar ambivalence to me and somewhat amused about this, seemingly indicating a felt gap between risks perceived by local services, versus how the space was used as a 'hang out'. Over the course of attending and participating in this group, it, along with many other services, was reduced, threatened with closure, and eventually moved online.

Leigh (35, white, straight, trans woman) participated in this group. But she expressed a level of frustration with local LGBTQ+ community groups, and specifically trans groups. In some ways Leigh repeats the very same risk ('too many problems') that she is seeking to avoid, highlighting 'rubbish' group effects, which are ultimately social, and structured by transphobia:

other people are too depressed and negative, they've got too many problems and they'll just go on about them. I don't want to do that, I want to have a laugh with my friends not hear the rubbish they're going through, constantly... So I tend to avoid trans groups on the whole, to be honest.

Leigh's interview was fun, punctuated with talk of shopping and the desire for things she doesn't have, alongside the planning of a 'better future' anticipated in awaiting the outcome of a job interview. Despite her recognisable resilience within the structural context of recession, Leigh's desires are likely to be rendered as wrong and inappropriate. Powerful ideas of the working-classes as wanting the wrong kinds of things, and as frivolous rather than frugal, act to hold the poor morally responsible for poverty, unemployment, and other structural inequalities. Stating that 'I feel like a lower-class person, because of the way I'm treated', Leigh also refused such judgement, attributing her unemployment to the recession, rather than as attached to her trans status: 'I'm not going to blame being trans, I'm just going to blame the recession …'.

A 'currency of comparisons' was navigated in community and commercialised scene spaces, often as overlapping venues transformed across day and night times. While interviewees spoke of being priced out of scene spaces, then part of the gentrified urban 'Gay as Now' upgrading, questions and costs of (in)accessibility were both material and moral. Scene spaces as lifestyle-generating leisure-orientated sites are in some ways exactly the kind of diverse entrepreneurial marketplaces to be celebrated and included. As well as a *cure for* austerity, as sites of care and community for queers, such venues were also positioned as the *cause of* austerity – as a moral excess. That these venues bore a heavy load was reflected in interviewees' mixed feelings, as conveyed by Leigh. The naming of scene spaces as 'dirty wee dives', 'slimy wee pubs', or 'wee holes' with 'boggin toilets', 'wet walls', and a 'crap karaoke singer' represented the gaps between 'Gay as Now' marketing and the deferral or failure of this. While Janice's sense that things were different in the past with price banding pre-existing contemporary mutual aid, pay-it-forward, pay-what-you-can initiatives (see Chapter 3), caution must be exercised about the potential romanticisation of poverty, and as a cure for corporate profit. Janice stated that 'when I first came to Newcastle and I was on the dole, at Rock 'n' Doris you didn't have to pay full price and you didn't have to prove you were on the dole, it was just "unwaged" and nobody challenged it …'. Despite this sense of access, exclusions between peers, produced in and by the LGBTQ+ community, have been complicit in enacting distinction, abjection, and otherness:

> ... there is that dynamic, there is a sexual dynamic in that for a lot of people. Scally lads and stuff in their tracky bottoms. Like people fetishize working-class guys, and working-class women I'm not sure about that, but I know that, for guys definitely.
>
> —Zac, 25, white, gay man

Imogen Tyler argues that affective abjection of classed and racialised groups represents a 'culturalization of poverty'. These representations mobilise fear, disgust, and abjection towards racialised and classed subjects, as materialised in the figure of the 'chav', or the 'bogus asylum seeker', and act to justify punitive welfare and border regimes.[14] For Tyler, these figures become 'ideological conductors' legitimising further retrenchment of the welfare state. Classed and racialised bodies are constituted in these everyday interactional scenes. They are 'fetishised' and sexualised as 'other', and Zac's uncertainty around the gendered dynamics of this itself points to the ongoing regulation of bodies, locating others as out of place, and legitimising a reduction to body parts, including in Fred's example as just 'disabled'.

These scenes highlight the intimate and sexual life of austerity, as a material and moral regime. Such a pushing in and out became a policy imperative within austerity regimes, but also a (parental) prerogative enacted within LGBTQ+ scenes.

Scene 2: Lesbian and gay parenting: securing social and educational capitals

> We're scary, you know? Yeah, we are both articulate and we've come from countries where we are used to having our rights and we know how to find out information for ourselves. The health visitors don't like us, they are afraid of us. We just look like the sort of people who could get really annoyed and make complaints and be a nuisance. And I know that's resource-based, but not everyone has that and that's just really unfair that we trade on that privilege.
>
> —Clare, 32, white, lesbian

From 2007 I spoke to lesbian- and gay-parented families across the UK; aware of the pressures on LGBTQ+ organisations, stretched by the changing socio-economic climate, I wanted to see how families fared. The UK's austerity period overlapped with the rolling-out of key legislation including the same-sex marriage Act of 2014, which extended the Civil Partnership Act 2004.[15] While the scenes of austerity and equalities might seem competing, they are linked in imagining discrete units – families, children, parents, citizens – as inhabiting their proper place and as replacing collective welfare. Queer-feminist analyses have been central to challenging the resourcing and idealisation of the family, including via state supports. In crisis times 'the family' is extended, with many of the same normative patterns becoming intensified in expectations, recognitions, and entitlements as the welfare state is cut back.

Clare has self-awareness and empathy but continues to 'trade on that privilege' nonetheless. Pity – rather than politics – often becomes a poor concession towards those who can't play this new parental game as effective choosers and consumers. These processes exist beyond Clare and the other middle-class parents I interviewed. And I am also implicated in these: I awkwardly realised my own proximity to and distance from becoming (mis-recognised as) a middle-class lesbian mum. In having a thyroid condition assessed I was referred to a local fertility centre. Although I answered 'no' from the outset in being asked if I wanted children, this question seemed to be on a loop, and one which seemed urgently linked to age – as someone potentially 'out of time'. I have ambivalent thoughts about this encounter as staff fully acknowledged my rela-tionship status, reassuring me that lesbian parents were on their (private) client list. I found myself pulled into a conversation about sperm donation, about global supplies and waiting lists, and I realised I'd been identified as a potential consumer, as one who'd maybe not realised all the services which she could now access. In reflecting on this, I wonder how my embodiment – from outright headshaking to head-at-an-angle curiosity – was misread and how such misreadings are a fundamental part of the parental 'trade'.

There are costs to such trade-offs, exchanged via institutional settings and in everyday conversations, often carried across time and place. But when I think about queer families, I think beyond the lesbian or gay couple who, having sought the right information, are more often praised as responsible rather than feared as scary. I grew up on a council estate in Glasgow in a single-parent family: I don't understand this as a scary situation, and the 'scary' estate was in fact differentiated. Young single-mothers have long been stigmatised (including by their working-class peers) and I bristle still when peers search for the go-to-story of family as finding-dad, or incorrectly anticipate a much older age to my mother (I understand this to be more than a commentary about her age). I grew up knowing that my mother's 'choices' about education, location, family, housing, and employment were deemed wrong, as a form of classed and sexual regulation and stigmatisation.[16] Parents have been thoroughly responsibilised for investing in and thus bringing forward children's futures, or admonished when unable to simply summon resources. The period of UK austerity politics, as a broad economic, political, and cultural formation and imagination, reached far beyond my own family, extending some of these histories into the present as wrong then and wrong now.

Middle-class queers may often recognise the injustice of trading on privilege, of being recognisable and legible to peers and institutions, as with Clare's reflection. Embodied dispositions of looking like the right 'sort of people' generate other affects, including discomfort and embarrassment. In some ways, Clare's experience represents wider contradictions in and as an 'austerity scene', whereby some can trouble systems and secure rights, while also being viewed as a nuisance. The Equality Act arguably created a legitimation of some lesbian and gay parents, like Clare, as no longer scary – yet there is a gap between legal entitlement and lived experiences. Clare and her partner have the resources to return to and bridge this gap, even viewing it as a personal triumph signalling their success as parents. This was not always true for other interviewees, some of whom had lived through different legal times, of court hearings, public shaming, and offensive media attention. I met lesbian mothers who had endured some of the first UK custody battles and been judged as unfit mothers. These memories and legacies endured and bumped up against new protections, and even celebrations, for the right kind of parents. Classed parenting practices can be unsettling, as well as just making 'good sense' as an everyday seemingly benign way of remaking class: who can deny the middle-class child the resources they need or deserve? In considering this I've felt distance from interviewees, upturning my own research claims on proximity or insider status. I was often told by more middle-class interviewees that I could choose, that I had a right to parent. In contrast, working-class interviewees often enthusiastically embraced my choice not to parent, counting costs and impacts, while at the same time evidencing their ability to cope and do parenting. Those who felt and faced the penalties of the reduced welfare state – being suspicious too of educational institutions as state structures implicated in re-making inequalities – could not be easily accommodated within or feel celebratory towards changing state formations.

Being a parent is resource-intensive. Often middle-class parents mentioned invested resources as evidence of their proper and deserving parental capacity. These parents pitched as respectable and decent, as thoughtful active planners, exercising parenting 'choices' (as opposed to those who just 'fell pregnant'), sometimes travelling globally to access fertility treatment or surrogacy. Working-class parents often had entirely different routes into parenting from their middle-class counterparts, mainly via previous heterosexual relationships, as routes to be re-evaluated as equally queer, rather than made wrong or straight.[17] Clare and her partner, Lisa (34, white, lesbian), told of simply being in the 'right place at the right time', where things happened 'accidentally'. However, their plans had involved deliberate timing and investment, including cross-continental travels. Lisa's self-description as the 'donor hooker' suggested a bit more effort in this 'huge process' than accident and luck alone.

Often middle-class deliberations – whether as routes to parenting or locational and schooling choices – were recognised and rewarded. Peter's account easily resonates with the 'families of choice' literature, where the material resources needed to make and mobilise individual choices are invisible.[18] In many ways such an idealised choice is exactly aligned to conservative and austerity discourses, relying on family, and doing it yourself. Peter's account is spatially – and materially – specific ('centred in London'), materialised in efforts of a 'like-minded' and well-resourced collective. What appears as a set of fluid possibilities would not be so without the finance to support it: such an arrangement would be cast as chaotic and deviant, simply by placing it within the context of a council estate as opposed to an urban collective. The scene described below is one of the affordances of inherited wealth, capitalised upon and extended in buying property at 'the right time':

> ... we were talking about this notion of 'urban family' ... in the sense that it's not necessarily blood relatives, it's the people who end up being significant in your life and who get involved ... We all shared a house hoping to do this hippy commune, bringing up our kids together ... And essentially, it feels like a collection of freaks who are not necessarily (laughter), they're not necessarily gay or straight, but they're just a bunch of quite interesting, bohemian people who have all become part of this extended, urban family, particularly centred in London.
>
> —Peter, 43, white, gay man

Diversity is coded as liberal middle-class knowingness spatialised in the specific cosmopolitan terrain of the inner city, and is positioned as fluid and open even though it rests upon the hoarding of resources. In both Peter's and Clare and Lisa's accounts naming character (scary, hippy, freaks) was used to name and displace privilege, as a fighting spirit or personality difference to be mobilised against homophobic sentiment. While Peter situates this as a collective difference to some extent ('a collection of freaks'), his urban family was protective and protected. Lisa's account of 'Stockbridge ladies' at the centre of queer parenting networks demonstrates the intersection of class and gender, encompassing values, lifestyles, and preferences, and creating a classed 'culture clash'. The classed exclusion which Clare and Lisa detailed functions covertly, constructed through seemingly individual *preferences*. Such preferences are rendered benign, while working to consolidate 'proper' (middle-class) parenting practices as natural and obvious. The queer picnic acts as a real 'eye opener' into enduring class dynamics and the navigation of 'mix', 'clash', and 'exposure':

Yes, it was just clashing values. All of a sudden there was this whole group of people and some of them felt that it was really okay to, you know, we're having a picnic in a park, to also be smoking in front of the children or leaving the children to it and beat each other up or whatever, and we're talking about... 'Oh it was so fun getting so drunk last night, snogging on the dance-floor, blah, blah, blah' (laughter). It's like 'Hey! Oh my God! Well maybe this isn't the best kind of chat for these kids to be around'. And then you had people on the other hand who were really trying to initiate games for the kids ...

—Clare, 32, white, lesbian

Ideas of 'cultural poverty' hinge on families', and often specifically mothers', ability to pass on the right kinds of cultural values and norms: austerity discourses heighten the divide and normative judgements between what makes a family (il)legitimate or (in)appropriate. In Clare and Lisa's account, what happened at a picnic came to represent a broader social story about proper parenting as educationally enhancing. What is learned here is the respective place of parents in classed hierarchies and the continual reinforcement of difference as deficit. In other groups, working-class parents might not return, with their absence reduced to a failure and one which the 'Stockbridge Ladies' will likely never feel:

Lisa: If there are more middle-class parents there and so the more working-class families, they don't come back ...

Clare: Yes. All parenting groups are like that, it's not just LGBT ones, so you'll get people saying about finding a group that matches, you know, not being the 'Stockbridge Ladies' or, you know ... Most parenting groups, you know, what I've heard, are very middle-class.

—Lisa, 34, white, lesbian and Clare, 32, white, lesbian

Working-class parenting was often framed by working-class interviewees matter-of-factly around that which 'just happened'. A liveable life is made up not only of the basic conditions required for surviving, such as shelter and medical care, but also, for instance, of the full range of intimate and caring relationships that a person requires to thrive. Instead of seeing working-class queer life as a failure, I imbue this with a worth and potentially as a queer departure from stories of investment and aspiration. Rather than exercising selective discernment of activities, residence, schools, friendships, and so on, working-class parents spoke instead of their children 'just being happy'. The value in proximity was gauged through access to friends, enjoying the company of others living locally, with local schools as the 'obvious' or only 'straight-forward' choice: '... I didn't think about it really. I'm not sort of a great pick and chooser' (Katerina, 52, white, lesbian). Like other parents from a similar background, Katerina was between ad hoc support systems, engaging with a patchwork of parental leave and benefits, reduced state support, and help from similarly placed, working-class families, neighbours, and friends. Working-class queers have long existed beyond state recognition or social (re) appraisal, while even in the context of austerity other queers have been able to ensure their own best interests.

Religion can act as a non-state structured mechanism benefit-ting working-class queers who don't have access to middle-class networks and capitals, and who exist outside of normative legi-bilities and 'protections'. Yet sexuality and religion have become over-represented as inevitable contradictions or distinct clashes, including within the 2010 Equality Act's framing of discrete 'pro-tected characteristics'.[19] The Metropolitan Community Church (MCC) was the example I turned to in 2010 as a queer case of religiosity, activism, and organisation, preceding supposedly progressive equality laws. The project, 'Making Space for Queer Religious Youth', navigated debates on religion as a conservative or transformative presence, coming to view queer religiosity as often offering a practical and long-standing buffer against austerity. Religion has long been seen as something to which people turn in times of crisis, as offering support, solace, and material resources in enabling a liveable life.[20]

Scene 3: Making space for queer identifying religious youth?

Where my research points to a queer path, this project seemingly disrupted that, pointing to secular assumptions about queer lives:

why was *I* researching religion? In some ways responding to the question is a bit like responding to the one about family, of filling-in-the-gap to allow a return to legibility, to trace the root or site of the problem. These problems are queer ones. And in many ways the place of religion in my life, or rather childhood, has been a queer presence and absence. As a child I attended the local Church of Scotland which sat between the working-class council estate I lived on and a relatively affluent area – which liked to distinguish itself by emphasising its prefix *Old* Drumchapel. We were led to church not necessarily by God but because a friend of a friend's mum had told my mum that her children got fed at church. The giro day – the day to collect state benefits from the post office – was on a Monday. Sundays were hungry days and the promise of soup and bread at church was enough of a lure. I loved going and soon joined in with the Brownies 101 pack – the Thursday night pack consisted of girls, like me, from the estate, and the other girls in the Tuesday night Brownie pack were from *Old* Drum-chapel. In recalling my time at church, people have pointed out that it seemed quite evangelical rather than Church of Scotland. Certainly, I remember jumping up and down in the pews, and lis-tening to vivid and animated sermons, which as a child I just took to be very good stories. At church I met Suzanne: we laughed at the choir of elders, stole 20 pences from the collection tray, and danced around a toadstool as Brownies. These were things I gladly did, in return for a bowl of soup, a harvest festival, a pantomime, a parade, and many a good song. Religion has been called 'the opium of the masses', a way to keep working-class people in their places; others have pointed to religious spaces as sites of social capital building and of getting-by.[21]

From my own ambivalent and partial experience, religious insti-tutions have long filled gaps, including those widened through austerity cuts in the post-welfare state. From 2010 I spent time in Metropolitan Community Churches (MCC) in the UK and the USA, interviewing young people across three MCC sites (Newcas-tle, Manchester, and London).[22] MCC describes itself as moving in the 'mainstream of Christianity' as an ecumenical organisa-tion affording individual congregations and pastors considerable autonomy with regards to sacraments, rites, and styles of worship.

MCC has a long history of activism and DIY cultures, including celebrating same-sex marriage and partnership before these became legally sanctioned. Gatherings have taken place in members' homes and borrowed premises, where long-term borrowing and making do is the norm. In a climate of austerity, different church spaces – and often unpaid staff – have been tasked with doing and resourcing community, persisting as precarious and ad hoc. This persistence was evident in the MCC Newcastle's slogan 'fabulous and beautiful', and the young people's talk of having a 'church family'.[23] Yet religious institutions and (counter)practices can also generate their own expectations and normativities, even as stand-ins for the state, or for family.

Abby and Estelle illuminate the lived experiences of religion in the context of austerity, responding to Sarah-Jane Page and Heather Shipley's (2020) question 'what is working-class queer religion?'[24] While religion and sexuality constitute flashpoints in Western socio-political discourse – amplified through the hostile environment of austerity regimes – there is much to learn in considering the intersection, rather than inevitable collision, in producing 'liveable lives' for working-class queer religious youth. In selecting Abby and Estelle I don't promote their unique difference or suggest that they are special cases – rather I frame these accounts as animating queer-feminist struggle around and beyond state solutions. Both Abby and Estelle were living on benefits, impacted by disability, and may well have been recognised as part of the group designated as NEETs – a derogatory term used to describe young people 'Not in Education, Employment, or Training'. Their stories highlight the limits of traditional family and the stretching of this via religion as 'church families'. As young people with disabilities they have cycled in and out of the workforce and been subject to benefit regulation, homelessness, hostility, and discrimination – as previously discussed in relation to Fred. Abby and Estelle embraced forms of activism and politicisation, including in anti-austerity protests and in their everyday lives, recalled by Abby as moments when she'd back up her wheelchair and 'wheel a few feet back'. Working-class queer religiosity is not singularly identifiable or expressed but rather articulated as a lived, complicated, and intimate practice, and the case of Abby and Estelle helps to query the privileging of the secular as a solution for queers. These cases return to and echo with and against the case of Farj (Chapter 4) and the cases of Asifa, Alisha, and Nneka (Chapter 6), who discuss the variously constraining and enabling aspects of religion, as also frequently conflated with race, with whiteness again rendered neutral, invisible, and as secular solution.

Abby

—31, white, omni pan-romantic, asexual, woman

I've known people who've been assaulted in the street for being disabled. Because the current war on disabled people in this country, when it comes to benefits, it's lower class versus lower class sort of thing, because 'they get more than us'. It's like an eye scratching game I find, sometimes. I just keep myself away from people who are negative ... wheel a few feet back!

Abby is a wheelchair user and described herself as pan-romantic and asexual. She experienced periods of short- and longer-term homelessness during her life, including after the divorce of her mum and dad when she was seven years old. She spoke of finally getting a house with her mum '... on a pretty rough estate, so some pretty bad things happened ...'. She was bullied at school as a result of her homeless status and moved between England and Wales. She explained that she'd found her own way in life, raising herself from a young age, as her mum had three jobs and so was often at work. As a young adult Abby again experienced homelessness, living with friends and later receiving a council house in a rural area. There she attended a local college for a few years but couldn't manage the distance between her house and college, due to her increasing illness ('...because of the amount of hills and stuff').

Given her geographical isolation, Abby then went to stay with her mum, which didn't work out. As a result, she returned to periods of staying with friends. During this time Abby enrolled on a college course in dancing '... because I wasn't disabled then ...'. She also worked in factories, but her disability gradually became worse, meaning 'that was the last job I had because I became too disabled to do it anymore'. She described this period of her life as '... just another bad experience. Because it isn't even one of the top five worst experiences in my life, I don't really tend to think about it too much ...'. Her health problems included chronic physical disabilities involving periods of hospitalisation, and she also managed mental health issues, which she attributed in part to childhood abuse. Notably, Abby's fear of homelessness persisted and impacted upon how she viewed intimate relationships: '... I would never give up my home to live with a partner because I've been homeless and I don't want to have to deal with that again, if the relationship breaks down'.

Abby described herself as a 'church hopper' and went between different churches, forming an 'eclectic spirituality', with Buddhist and Pagan leanings. She'd experienced religion as a young person, which in practice meant that Abby had attended Brownies ('To me, to be quite honest, the only time I used to go to church as a kid was when we had the flag carrying thing with the Brownies, every month or so. I never really felt connected with Christianity as a person'). A friend then introduced her to Buddhism at the age of 16 and she selected the parts of it that resonated and that she 'wanted to keep', before joining a church in Manchester on moving in with a friend who attended. She described this as a mixed space with a nice community, encompassing different beliefs, and positions this as buffering, pragmatic, and protective rather than acquisitive:

> I'm not saying I pick and mix the best bits of religion, I find things that work for me ... I just really liked the fact that there was structured services for us and the way we do things like meditation and sing hymns and stuff but obviously not your garden variety Christian church style ... So there's people you can rely on, who you see a lot. I think that is probably the biggest part of going to church for me, is the fact that it's a community and it's there for you.

Abby was conscious of the ways a 'pick and mix' approach to religion might be dismissed, but enjoyed the inclusive practices within the church, including a sense of equality and access as a wheelchair user in the round open plan room:

> Basically, we sit in a circle ... I feel when you go into a church, like a Christian church, all sat in rows, that you're sat there, all supposed to be looking up at the big man and to me I like the fact that we sit rounder and not looking up at anything partic- ularly. To me, I think being in a round setting with a table that's our height, and you don't look up at anything is kind of like ... it puts the focus more back on the people for their beliefs, rather than an external force for it.

Abby was conscious of the increasingly hostile climate towards people with disabilities, directly relating this to the curtailment of benefits as a 'war on disabled people'. Regularly having to navigate taken-for-granted everyday space, via road bumps and ramps, she spoke of how 'every day of my life is a challenge as a disabled person in a wheelchair'. Such challenges persisted in inaccessible LGBTQ+ scene space usually located underground or upstairs:

> a lot of the clubs were at underground level, so I couldn't go to them even if I wanted to. I've never tried to go out to the gay scene here because, to be quite honest, I was turned off by the fact that it was inaccessible in other places as well. Not just the whole big, 'We're here and we're queer' thing, it is as well often the fact that they're not very accessible because they're stuck on the edges of towns where people can ignore it.

Working-class religiosity may be the attempted practice of – or entry into – a place and existence without bumps. Abby and Estelle are able to strategically and pragmatically 'mix' although there is hesitancy in aligning with an acquisitive 'pick and mix' consumer logic, often unashamedly embraced by middle-classes. Impor- tantly, however, they are able to identify as religious without the racialised weight that this takes on for other interviewees, such as Farj (Chapter 4) or Alisha (Chapter 6) even in their dis-similar narratives of religious pragmatism.

Estelle
—25, white, queer-lesbian, woman

Estelle had experienced sporadic living and working conditions, moving from low-paid employment through long-term sickness benefit and unemployment, and routinely navigated social stigma. Like Abby, Estelle described her family circumstances as 'complicated' and 'abusive', and was estranged from her family. She was also badly bullied at school, despite her mum and grandmother having made sure she attended the local Catholic church as a way of ensuring entry to the better school.[25] Her schooling experiences were often bad, re-told as a time of 'verbal and physical bullying'. In stark contrast to the circulating representation of benefits claimants as apathetic and lazy 'scroungers', she had been enrolled on a nursing programme, but could not manage this alongside her health condition.

Estelle described how over the past two years her life had 'ground to a halt' because of her illness: she was still involved in queer-religious community yet conscious, like Abby, of differing entry points and exits (also echoing with earlier accounts of parenting realities):

> I think they [women] tend to have less money as well because they are more politically minded and maybe less likely to be in high flying jobs and things like that ... there's a women's night, a lesbian night that always ends at midnight, it's out of town and is in Whalley Range, and it's really funny because just as I'm getting into it, dancing, it's like 'Vhoom!' and everything stops and everyone's gone home because the babysitter's waiting (laughter).

Like Abby, Estelle had clear opinions about the LGBTQ+ community, seeing herself as a 'queer lesbian', who was actively involved in anti-austerity activism with friends. Estelle described tensions between being queer, being Christian, and being young, viewing her religious practice as actively 'seeing the good in people. I think God is the good in people in a way.' The sense of queer-religion was materialised in-between physical locales, and Estelle had found some refuge in what she described as a fairly 'conservative church environment'. She compared and contrasted this with her 'queer bubble' in ad hoc MCC space, as more diverse and mixed, but where people 'dare to talk about like gay stuff and race and stuff'. The presence of a woman vicar, and a cross-generational and ethnically diverse congregation, allowed for a more 'liberal' and 'cool' orientation:

> There's a lot of queer politics out there, but in my sort of bubble, it's very much about having a lot of consideration about a lot of different intersectionalities about people's race and gender and age and ability and all this kind of stuff which is really respected. So there's that sort of community element that you can also find in spiritual places that I think everyone's aiming towards a common good ... and I think that is in queer circle and in more spiritual, church circles, both have those sort of social aims about their groups.

In contrast to depictions of working-class life as lacking, dependent, and dis-invested, both Estelle and Abby express a range of queer-class collectivised cultures, surpassing an individualised narrative of success and choice. In the opening excerpt to this chapter, Estelle recounts her involvement in anti-austerity protest as joyful, creative, and public. The anti-capitalist sentiments mobilised by Estelle are echoed in her insights into and alignment with 'intersectionality' as a politicised vocabulary alive in her 'queer bubble', rather than as wholly confined to academia, or even as academic outreach. Feminist-queer theory must sit with queer-feminist practice to articulate some of the everyday struggles in making a life in the midst of structures that continue to render presences out of place, and futures uncertain. There is 'a lot of queer politics out there': class and religion intersect in these lived realities, and as (anti-)austerity scenes, which challenge the austerity of imagination in separating queer/religion.

CONCLUSION: BEYOND AN AUSTERITY OF IMAGINATION

This chapter has explored queers and austerity across three intersecting scenes weaving in state policy and everyday inequality as intimate disruptions. Queer-feminist research on austerity and precarity asks what justice can mean and look like, whether looking to the experience of perpetual crisis after 9/11 and the potential to forge new solidarities, or to the differential effects of structural inequality in the wake of the 2008 Financial Crisis.[26] The austerity scenes re-imagined here, as a return back to and forward through specific yet continued times, involve being present 'in the field', carrying and *doing* data across time and place (see Chapter 4). Austerity speaks to the experience of contingency, insecurity, and impermanence, as belonging to queer times. Different types of queer life persist through austerity, where forms of middle-classness make life more liveable for queers. However, such queer times also witness the making of working-class queer life as liveable, including in and against the everyday scenes of LGBTQ+ community spaces, family life, and religious practices. There is more to (sexual) life than that ascribed by austerity politics. Chapter 6, *Queer Anachronisms: Working-Class Lesbians out of Time and Place*, looks back on 20 years of research on working-class lesbian lives in the UK illuminating contemporary debates on 'real life' at the intersection, or hyphenation, of queer-lesbian, as per Estelle's usage.

6

Queer Anachronisms: Working-Class Lesbians Out of Time and Place

I use dyke, I use queer, I use other words as well. But 'what is your identity?' I would say lesbian. I suppose that was my first politicisation ... using the word lesbian was a hugely politicising thing for me that I kind of picked up through feminism, I think.
—Sally, 56, white, lesbian

The lesbian as a figure might even overinherit queerness: in a heteropatriarchal world there might be nothing odder, or more striking, than women who have as their primary sexual and life partners other women. Lesbians: queer before queer.
—Sara Ahmed, *Living a Feminist Life*, 2017: 224[1]

Still, with the dearth of data on working-class lesbians, the book may appeal to scholars in lesbian studies who are looking for data on class.
—Review of *Working-Class Lesbian Life*, 2007

One of my long-term goals across projects has been both to represent queer working-class life and to imbue it with worth. The accounts of working-class queers are more than data. Interviewees have made me laugh again and again, in turn laughing with me, and sometimes at my own errors as interviewer. I've quoted interviewees at length, sometimes expecting them to do the lengthy work of speaking back and against abstract theorisation that I've struggled to counter. Reclaiming real life can mean telling particular stories; laughing together can become evidence of the authentic connection between interviewees and interviewers, or of anti-pretentious sentiment mobilised against middle-class propriety. Working-class realities were often spoken about matter-of-factly, and in writing *Working-Class Lesbian Life* I made a pitch and effort at including this reality. I tried to get everything on the page, writing across family background, schooling, work experiences, neighbourhoods and communities, leisure activities, scene spaces, and intimate relationships. I charted identifications formed in childhood through an awareness of parental employment and unemployment, communal solidarity, financial hardship, and difference. But these real signs of authentic working-classness – such as council house residency, voting Labour, union involvement, community networks – are always fractured.

Describing these realities can mean coming out and claiming a place for lived experiences, as queer continues to grapple with 'real life'.[2] In balancing their words and my words – and the words of other academics – things compete and become un-disciplined. I've rushed to put everything, or everyone, on the page. And I've been warned that the page may end up too messy, or too basic, not elevated to an academic fit. Queer has claimed a mess and mis-fit too, but as subversion rather than stuckness.[3] The problem of 'real life' empiricism can become an academic criticism that data is 'undertheorised', and, as one reviewer of *Working-Class Lesbian Life* supposed, that research is only *potentially* useful as a database that others could use or theorise from: as 'scholars … looking for data on class' (see above extract). In prioritising interviewees' voices, I ran the risk of not being academic enough, where the book '… offers some new data but frustratingly little theory … in favour of a series of chapters that attempt to cover the various contexts of lived experiences for Taylor's narrators'. This review conveys the respective weight between knowing or doing, and between data and theory. There *is* weightedness in selecting and conveying 'lived experience', including lived experiences of sexism, racism, and classism. The experience of others may be cast as authenticity and evidence, appropriated and included, while also pitted against theorisation or intellectualisation, as queer theory returns to white men. But the review weighs productively too, as usefulness attempted over and over again, mis-used, disputed, and messed with. Queer method works in knowing where we stand, where we are going, and who we are taking with us over again.[4]

My archiving, through 20 years of data collection and theorising real life, has felt quite big, or, rather, quite stretched, but I also hold onto the potential of, through, and as 'little theory'. Over time, I've engaged with a broad range of queer-feminist and class theories (see Chapter 7), and in often being out of time and place, I've tried to combine theories of identity and performativity with feminist sociological perspectives on class. In writing *Working-Class Lesbian Life* I diverged from two important UK-based empirical studies on LGBTQ+ lives in the late 1990s and early 2000s: Gill Dunne's *Lesbian Lifestyles* (1997) and Jeffrey Weeks, Brian Heaphy, and Catherine Donovan's *Same Sex Intimacies* (2001).[5] In some ways these studies were also empirically placing lesbians as 'queer before queer', embedded in changing political times. 'Lesbian lifestyle' and 'families of choice' literature often idealised difference rather than locating this as classed, nonetheless positively affirming alternative economic and domestic structures beyond heteronormativity. Looking back, I think about how my 'data collection', 'data analysis', 'data presentation' was and is categorised as an academic sorting process – and how both the researcher and the research(ed) may be too much or too little as working-class lesbians. Going back to and through these patterned realities can work against disciplining locations and social structures, as an ever-present risk in still being out of time and place. I'm still part of a feminist-queer community, looking for and through data on class, collectivising and politicising queer-class archives, including the ones I've created, returned to, and written through, and as part of my lived experience. While '[t]he lesbian appears as an abject figure we were all surely happy to have left behind', she, like me, nonetheless 'continues to stalk queer', including through 'failed' projects, books and data.[6]

In this chapter I re-read the case of the lesbian as an imperative to think about bodies out of time and place. The previous chapter ended with the accounts of Estelle and Abby, who used, changed, and mixed terms such as 'lesbian-identified', 'queer-lesbian', 'pan-romantic', and 'asexual', as reflected in Sally's 'other words' above. Individual choices and identifications sit alongside social worlds, as weighted in the question 'What is your identity?' What's the use in returning to a term like 'lesbian' which has become so weighted in refusal, disappointment, and anachrony? The lesbian is old-fashioned, out-of-time, always and already represented as an 'unsophisticated, essentialist' political position. If left off, discarded by, yet still carrying or overinheriting 'queer', how might lesbian presence move us back to and forward through queer-left politics? Feminists have produced a considerable body of work that challenges the construction of queer theory as the new or better replacement for feminist thinking.[7] But if lesbian studies is always understood to be a sub-field, marginal to the field of queer theory, then the striking force of lesbian, as 'queer before queer', may be reduced. What weight do we expect 'The Lesbian' to carry as a queer, intersectional figure whose 'real life' may be oddly forgotten, appropriated, and (de)politicised? In this chapter I reflect across 20 years of research on working-class lesbian lives in the UK, situated in relation to three empirical cases, as well as the case of the research(er) coming out of class and race categories. The 'queer anachronisms' that lesbians inhabit and articulate help bridge the terrain of queer theory, class studies, and feminism as intersectional, allied forces, always implicated in the (un)making of racialised, gendered, and classed structures.

Scholarship from lesbians of colour has been central to queer theory's development – long addressing intersections of gender, race, class, and sexuality – yet this work has been sidelined and whitened.[8] The Combahee River Collective was a collective of Black lesbian feminists created in 1975 and emerging against the racism in women's movements and the sexism in Black movements. From the outset, the collective emphasised intersectional politics as emerging from lived experiences:

> [W]e are actively committed to struggling against racial, sexual, heterosexual, and class oppression, and see as our particular task the development of integrated analysis and practice based upon the fact that the major systems of oppression are interlocking. The synthesis of these oppressions creates the conditions of our lives.[9]

The collective acknowledged the long-term work involved in political struggle as a practised commitment, likely fractured by disagreements and conflicts, but pursued nonetheless: 'we know we have a very definite revolutionary task to perform and we are ready for the lifetime of work and struggle before us'.[10] Black lesbian feminism has actively pursued an intersectional politics challenging the false universalism of 'womenhood', as well as ideas of a united 'queer umbrella'. Gloria Anzaldúa, for example, expressed affinity *and* scepticism towards 'queer', as she also noted white academics' usage of queer in constructing '... a false unifying umbrella which all queers of all races, ethnicities and classes are shoved under'.[11] The unstated whiteness of the queer body in the nation, the family, the scene, and the classroom – and often in queer and feminist theory itself – has been critiqued, with some early and long-term contributors highlighted in Chapter 7.[12]

More than three decades on from the formation of the Combahee River Collective, contributors to *Out of Time and Place: Interrogating Silences in Queerness/Raciality*[13] again highlighted intersections of race and queerness, where the 'war on terror' following 9/11 continues in everyday state-sanctioned racisms. The racial privilege of white Western homonormativity acts to push others out of place, as explored in relation to 'Rainbow Europe' and other formations of the progressive state (Chapter 4). At the same time, racism continues as structural and everyday discrimination, including in queer scene spaces, while the realisation of community or scene spaces as white, like national or disciplinary spaces, does not in itself undo whiteness.[14] Indeed, such processes may extend whiteness as a personalised moment of self-consciousness or individualised guilt. Rather than individualising these movements of self-awareness – as per contemporary 'unconscious-bias training' as standing in for the contemporary queer-feminist classroom – my intention is to think through 'the lesbian' as a queer anachronism interrupting feminist, political, and even research, arrivals.

Nearly two decades after starting on the project *Working-Class Lesbian Life*, and coinciding with the writing of this book, the 2021 film *Rebel Dykes*[15] was released. With curiosity, I watched those who'd used the terms 'lesbian' and 'dyke', only with disdain and suspicion, moving to celebratory positions, announcing their appreciation of the film. I felt some frustration and seduction in processes of visibility, appropriation and authenticity, and in being pulled back to a time and place that was and wasn't 'mine'. *Rebel Dykes* powerfully demonstrates the rebellious feminisms of the 1980s – as riotous, angry, and naughty – and, to quote from the film, 'long before queer or riot grrrls'. In many ways, lesbian-feminist, radicalesbian, or rebel dyke community has always been characterised as much by division, tension, and difference as by unity, solidarity, and coalitions: the film highlights long-standing feminist resistance against sex-gender essentialisms *and* investments in the category of 'women', including as a 'necessary fiction'.[16]

The 'sex wars' of the 1980s and 1990s resonate with the re-emergence of sex-gender wars in the contemporary context, particularly in terms of transphobia, where *Rebel Dykes* highlights the histories of transmisogyny. Shannon Keating argues '... the word "lesbian" has carried such a deeply uncool connotation for so long – sometimes for terrible reasons (ugly, old-fashioned, essentialist stereotypes) and sometimes for extremely legitimate ones (a history of transmisogyny) – that it's worth considering if making the term cool is something we should really want at all'.[17] Contemporary TERF wars – an abbreviation signalling 'trans-exclusionary radical feminist' positions from trans-inclusive feminism – can be situated across time and place, highlighting divisions within feminisms, as ever-responsive to political changes, including right-wing conservatism.[18] In this respect, new-old battles can be charted in sex wars and intersectionality wars, as changing and emergent political directions into which lesbian politics also re-surface.[19] When 'lesbian' is used as a rallying cry for right-wing conservative social projects – assimilating good gays, lesbians, and bisexuals[20] into the mainstream life of the nation and the family – we need to be mindful and suspicious of trans exclusions, which also elide the possibility of trans lesbian life.

I return and re-read lesbian life as a queer person, not to return to an assumed essentialist 'real woman' or 'authentic lesbian' position. I do so precisely to challenge such notions and to illustrate a variety of lesbian lives beyond white cis imaginings. As Jules Gill-Peterson argues, trans lesbians contribute to anti-TERF thinking, effectively connecting lesbian and trans studies, '... making transness as much an empirical *increase* to their ranks, rather than an existential threat'.[21] Rather than effacing the word 'lesbian' from 'queer' or 'trans', I join others in deploying these terms in dialogue, including in the interrogation of '... racist, transphobic, and colonialist assemblages of systemic violence and discrimination', in the hope of keeping queer theory '... open and in constant dialogue with its own limitations'.[22]

Queer spaces are racialised to maintain boundaries, and white research(ers) can be complicit here, maintaining the structural invisibility of whiteness. 'Coming out' has its own normative patterns, as a revelation or confession, as a sign of the realised self who announces, authenticates, and fulfils their identity. An individualisation of identity – as ours – can privatise and depoliticise as *only our*, or *not our*, issue. Whiteness becomes the issue which doesn't name itself, as a research presence, embodied by me as researcher and reflected in what have been predominantly white samples. Quoting Peggy McIntosh's (1989) statement on white privilege as '... an invisible package of unearned assets that I can count on cashing in each day, but about which I was "meant" to remain oblivious', Catherine Crisp[23] notes how diversifying samples doesn't solve the problem of whiteness, and neither do singular confessions or moments of 'coming out' as a white person. Data analysis can extend confessions or acknowledgement as continual practice:

> One of the dangers within feminist circles is a kind of acknowledgment without analysis. Often, feminists are willing to acknowledge privilege, but the analysis of that privilege is lacking. There might be a recognition of a lack of racial and ethnic diversity, especially among white lesbians, but it sometimes results in simple confessions of needing more 'outreach' to lesbians of color.[24]

Going back to research, to data, to real life, means reaching back through questions of positionality, and re-evaluating my past self, and past work, as more than just 'outreach'. My whiteness sits as an invisible package even within the learning, knowing, and naming of queer of colour scholarship in the feminist classroom (Chapter 7). As a white person, I do not fear or face being the victim of racism. And, like Crisp, as '... a white person, I am not expected to speak for my entire race but as a lesbian, I am often asked "How do lesbians ...?" I am rarely the only white person in certain settings, but I am often the only lesbian. I am not known as the "white professor", but my students tell me I have been referred to as the "lesbian professor".[25] Invoking the classroom or the research encounter as a space of possibility and dialogue does not render everything or everyone equally present – there are still absences in my research. When I think about my younger and older selves – carried here in going between data across time periods – I think about the weight of evidence, of gathering, being, and doing data. In holding onto pasts, I try to mobilise these, including beyond the one researcher who does 'outreach', finds a 'dearth of data', and then knows. Rather than dismissing my past self as unknowing in contrast to the 'knowing' researcher I've become, I want to think about reaching across time and place, to consider how whiteness still evades and escapes a location. I want to think about the mis-location of 'lesbian' as in-her-place in lesbian studies, and to think instead about being and doing interdisciplinarity as a repeated queer stretch and a queer, gendered, racialised labour.

Working-class lesbians can be thought of as a queer case, enmeshed in real-life intersectional inequalities, while often being out of time and place. The words of Asifa, Alisha, and Nneka generate responses – a necessity to write out and write back politicised academic vocabularies of intersectionality and queerness, in and as a lesbian feminism which includes lesbians of colour and trans lesbians.[26] As part of a constant dialogue with the queer left, our 'first politicisation(s)' are revived and kept alive. I carry queer-class project(s) into the present, through the past, remembering successes and failures, including the failure of a linear, completed project, as done and ready to be deposited in the archive. Going back can mean feeling stuck – 'she's *still* researching working-class lesbians!' But this return is meant as a way to become at least partially unstuck. It is not meant as a 'queering from above', whereby we, as queers, reach the truth or finalise the research(ed) via incorporation of queerer subjects. We are all implicated in processes of classing, racialisation, and gendering, and the hope is that queer-feminist research – as a return and revisioning – can be explicit about this, as well as its own faults, edits, and (re)interpretations in making a queer case: whose real life appears in and out of time and place as queer anachronisms?

LESBIANS OF COLOUR, TRANS LESBIANS, QUEER LESBIANS

Asifa was interviewed in 2002, yet her account resonates with Alisha's and Nneka's gathered nearly two decades later. Despite the temporal lapse, Asifa, Alisha, and Nneka echoed one another in talking about British racism as an ever-present hostile environment. In putting Asifa's, Alisha's, and Nneka's accounts alongside each other my purpose is not to conflate, but rather to highlight what is held in common and what constitutes a pushing-out across time and place. Across accounts, the key dates of 9/11 and 7/7 were mentioned as reigniting so-called wars on terror and hostility towards outsiders, asylum seekers, and migrants continually placing them, their families, and communities as not yet 'arrived'. Across time and place, Asifa, Alisha, and Nneka talked about navigating borders and belonging, of international, national, and regional identities, punctuated in a climate of austerity, (post)Brexit nationalisms, and the global COVID-19 pandemic. As racialised within different and similar contexts, they become 'space invaders' in moving between communities, as Scottish-English-British, South Asian, Nigerian, LGBTQ+, while not singularly or straightforwardly fitting normative categories.[27] Their families' intergenerational migration from and into different classed and caste contexts complicates the binary between the Global North/South, and the story of working-classness as white; their code-switching as bilingual women complicates the recognition of local accents as only classed (resonating with the mis-reading of Jaslene as 'rude', reported in Chapter 3).

Asifa

> I always felt at the bottom of the hierarchy, or that I felt I was being put at the bottom, I don't know that I necessarily felt that I was at the bottom.
>
> —Asifa, 29, South Asian, lesbian

Asifa was interviewed in the changing Northern working-class city of Manchester with both 'industrial' and 'Gay as Now' past-presences. I met Asifa in the autumn of 2002, around one year after 9/11, which she talked about as a defining moment of politicisation, with racist encounters a part of her everyday landscape, including in queer spaces. In recognising everyday agency in bumping up against hostile institutions, people, and places, as opposed to spectacular or celebrated moments of queer life, it is possible to recognise Asifa as a 'queer' and a 'rebel dyke'. Yet Asifa continued to be positioned through racist-sexist stereotypes as someone caught-between-two-worlds, presumed to be religiously weighted, submissive, passive, and oppressed.[28]

Asifa and I arranged to meet in a local LGBTQ+ centre which had allowed us to use an empty room as an interview location. As a 'queer researcher' doing interviews with the 'queer(ly) researched' I still have a sense of the often-precarious ways of occupying public space. Often LGBTQ+ venues may themselves be precarious, underfunded, and ever re-located (e.g. Glasgow Women's Library; see Chapter 2). On arriving in the local community space, I realised we were its main occupants – with only myself, Asifa, and a worker in the venue on the early afternoon weekday. Around us were posters about HIV/AIDS, safe sex, and condom usage (see Chapter 5 on LGBTQ+ space as a post-'Gay as Now' austerity scene). We read the venue as men's space, even when occupied by three women; I didn't have to notice or read the space as white, and missing this then and saying it now offers no easy resolve. The LGBTQ+ centre sat off-centre from the main scene space of Canal Street and felt cold and rather sad on that day. In retrospect, and in consideration of the loss of such venues during what would become intensified periods of cutbacks and austerity, I feel a loss for spaces such as these – even the cold ones with pamphlets warning of risky behaviours. Yet the risks faced by working-class queers might not be the ones posted on community noticeboards as action points or (health) checks. To be in-between heightened commercialisation as the gay-as-now trend moved to 'post-gay' digital spaces, is to be awkwardly located, including in the outreach provision for 'at risk' groups medicalised in funding agendas.

I still have a clear sense of meeting Asifa that day, planning and anticipating our interview. I have a sense still of the words, thoughts, and actions held in common – and the ways our experiences departed. Asifa's account included experiences of racism, educational limitation, and feminist politics, which featured as intimate sore points, as well as refused hierarchies. Asifa left home at 18 years, viewing education as a possible legitimate ('legal') way of resisting familial expectations around marriage, domesticity, and care. In pursuing education, she became estranged from both her family and the educational system, where schoolteachers were eager to see her as just another poor Asian woman 'caught between two cultures', as Asifa put it. Her story challenges essentialist notions of identity, including those produced by educational authorities – as incidents of failure and victimhood. It also complicates becoming 'lesbian' and the story of 'big city' queer existence or self-realisation via university attendance.[29] Asifa's 'coming out' story involved coming up against intersecting inequalities, of race, class, gender, sexuality, caste, and religion. Her first sexual relationship was a heterosexual one, which is a much-shared experience with other working-class queers (Chapter 5). Asifa described her family's horror at hearing how, as a Muslim woman, she was dating a Hindu boy; a decision which she didn't regret, except that he was a 'prat'. Another trope of LGBTQ+ identity, as fixed, always known, even if hidden or masked, is laid aside through a matter-of-fact non-regretful pragmatism. This reminds us of lesbian life as a re-direction and re-orientation, rather than an essential state of being.

Asifa's mum and dad moved from Pakistan to Britain in the '60s for a 'better life'. It was the rurality of her parents, recognised as being from a particular rural village in Pakistan ('… Like the back waters of a mountain village …'), known within the local Manchester Muslim community, that placed them on the periphery of a group already on the outside. For Asifa, this reality complicated homogenising racist slurs ('Nowadays you just get called the typical "Paki" by other people 'cause they don't necessarily understand the subtleties of that, the class system …'). Asifa also described classed and racialised expectations from teachers and a sense of being different and excluded from respectable Northern white working-class communities. Alongside a sense of such embedded exclusions, Asifa nonetheless expressed a sense of class solidarity and a politics, describing the middle-class communities that she moved through with disdain and anger. She spoke of education as a constant uphill struggle, as having to navigate a 'steep learning curve', and one that often cycled back to memories of her schooling days and to feeling patronised and poor. 'Poor kids' can hold onto past memories as significant senses. These memories can be defiant rather than deferent, guiding ways of becoming otherwise:

> ... 'you've been brought up in a Muslim family, of course you'll want to leave, it's shite and oppressive towards women'. That's really horrible to hear about your family ... the whole kind of thing about people saying 'Well you know what Asian families are like', from teachers and stuff ... they'd say 'You'll never be able to survive it' ... I think they just assumed it was the same old stuff that 'torn between two cultures and wanting independence'. Of course there were elements of that but it wasn't, I don't know anybody who's ever left home for those reasons 'cause they're so abstract really. It was *horrible* when I was growing up, it wasn't something I could bear but I don't think any of them understood that. They went with their assumptions.

Asifa experienced higher education as a 'first generation' entrant, ambivalently feeling her way through the university system with 'lots of waivers' and a six-month suspension period. Her account is framed by survival, a strategy she developed over time through getting by in middle-class settings, without resorting to what would have been her childhood solution, to 'kick the shit out of them'. Her sense of 'street culture', as political resistance, is again complicated by the institutional and interpersonal realms where such realities are refused and pathologised. In framing her political consciousness, Asifa spoke about her homelessness, and of accessing a women's refuge. This was conducive as an introduction to feminist practices, but it was not always felt as a 'safe space', with differences between women played out, re-ordering the hierarchies lived in and against. As Asifa explained, 'there weren't any lesbians ... in the Asian women's refuge' but she felt nonetheless that it 'opened doors'. Asifa's example of what these intersections looked and felt like is telling of the class boundaries re-made, including in feminist Asian women's spaces:

> ... in addition to describing myself as working-class I'd also describe myself as Asian, so I've always felt 'Well is it because I'm Asian, is it because I've been exposed to such a different culture that I don't survive?' But I knew that middle-class Asian people do really well in those environments and I've realised I don't relate to them as much as I do working-class people from those backgrounds ... When I went to the Asian women's project they didn't accept that those kinds of difficulties which I described happened in Asian families ... they said 'Oh well your parents aren't well educated that's why they wont accept this'... they were all these middle-class women who came from really well off backgrounds in Pakistan and they were running this project, and her daughter was getting all excited about going to uni and I was sitting there and she was saying 'Your mum too could be like this' and I was thinking 'Right'. I think there is an element of class in it ... why they felt my family was behaving how they were 'cause that's the way working-class families behaved, and how working-class Asians behaved, how the 'illiterates' behave ...

Asifa had a place of sorts within the feminist project, but one which expected her to regret, forget and escape her background, even as it was continually invoked: she was reassured that her future could be secured if 'others' – in this case her mother – could be like the middle-class women in the group. Nearly 20 years later, and amidst some LGBTQ+ families achieving legitimacy and entitlement, the story of a particular freedom for, or freedom from, *certain* families persists as deeply classed and racialised.

Alisha

So you're just like constantly having to explain yourself or be an anomaly or, but you kind of get used to that. Like of course you do. I mean I don't want anyone's pity because I'm like the only brown person in the room. Like it's been like this for decades. How do you think I get through every day? (laughs)

—Alisha, 39, South Asian, lesbian

The mattering of class is layered by the mattering of race and religion, sedimented in personal, social, and global events, and impossible to cast off. Like Asifa, Alisha highlighted race and class as having a continuous impact on her early life, growing up in a Scottish city in a 'really conservative' South Asian working-class Sikh family. Interviewed in 2019, she described class as a key orientating factor in her early life, realising and feeling her 'exceptionally poor' background from a young age, where money and food were constant worries, barely alleviated by a free school meal which brought its own stigma. Of a similar age to what Asifa is now, Alisha also remembered 9/11 as a still pivotal presence, 'getting mislabelled and miscategorised as Muslim' through racist hypervisibility and invisibility, where '... before 9/11, especially in Scotland, people were just lumped together as being Asian, whereas since 9/11 there's been more of a distinction'.

There are national and local differences, which mobilise distinction as place-based character, as cosmopolitan 'big city' claims or as everyday provincialisms. Alisha makes a geographical link between different Northern English cities, but her account also locates racism in the everyday, resisting the story of Scotland as a different kind of place, one of 'belligerent friendliness' which expresses a 'no problem here' position.[30] Making connections across the UK and between specific places (Glasgow, Newcastle, Manchester, Liverpool) and characteristics, Alisha invokes provincial cosmopolitanism within transitional and migrant working-class communities:

I think if you spend enough time on the streets of Glasgow you find lots of people who are, you know, I call it a kind of belligerent friendliness (laughter). And it's a nosiness about other people and a willingness to intervene in the environment around you, positively or negatively (laughs) ... And definitely an intolerance to something that might sound like bullshit ... but I think that's then a working-class thing. I think there are lots of working-class cities and communities in the UK ... if I was in Newcastle or Manchester, you know, or Liverpool, I might be saying exactly the same things. So maybe it's just these post-industrial cities with working-class communities that have been in transition, that have had migrant populations arrive so are hyper-diverse ...

Going on to describe this as a 'strange mixture' – often one not celebrated as the right kind of sophisticated 'big city' cosmopolitanism – Alisha described how the area that she grew up in had nonetheless changed and had pushed out working-class people of colour.

These structural processes of racism and classism are place-making and stick in particular ways. And yet it is Alisha who, like Asifa, is seen as stuck 'between two worlds', with religiosity inevitably positioned as entirely conservative. Alisha spoke about navigating these go-to stories and, like Asifa, identified as atheist, but spoke of the importance of religion in her life and the proximity of the Gurdwara as a prevailing presence in her childhood and adulthood. Unlike Asifa, who was estranged from her family, Alisha returned to Scotland from England in part to care for her elderly mum ('... we know that women disproportionately get lumbered with pastoral care'). In navigating her childhood landscape, new 'aunties' were encountered – and avoided – in old streets, as those who knew who she was because they knew her mum.

Such relations stretching across time are ones unlikely to feature as 'families of choice' in queer stories of locational and relational networks (Chapter 5) – yet they mean and do more than simply constraining or enabling 'outness'. Alisha generally avoided public displays of affection, as such displays could have consequences beyond her own 'outness' ('I do have some designated danger zones around temples and other places of religious worship ...'). Rather than seeing such places as just sites of trouble – as figured through homonationalist claims which present the state as saving queers by punishing racialised others – it is important to take into account other protections denied, offered, and pragmatically engaged with. Specifically, Alisha knows the Gurdwara and the aunties as buffering forces within the community, materialised as

sources of support for her mother. Against this specific – and curtailed – form of support sat a persisting sense of extended racisms
as the real 'danger zone'.

Nneka

> I know I'm going into a lot about race and stuff. It's just like trans
> and race is like bread and butter to me. It's like both are things
> that are important.
>
> (Nneka, 23, mixed race, pansexual lesbian, trans woman)

I met Nneka in the summer of 2019, and the complication of community, kinship, migration, and belonging continued as a link
across time and place, resonating with both Alisha's and Asifa's
accounts. In this, the story and sentimentality of Scotland as either
not-diverse, the 'white high-lands',[31] or supremely diverse by virtue
of Scottish difference, was troubled by non-cosmopolitan 'strange
mixtures' and provincial dis-placements. My return to the 'capital
of the Highlands', Inverness, connected my meeting with Nneka to
meeting the Rural Lesbian Group – in a 'posh hotel' – two decades
earlier. I remembered how the group organiser had told me that
some women found it hard to travel across the vast and varied
area to come to the monthly meetings and how others had felt
intimidated by the venue, chosen as a 'safe space'. I hadn't been in
Inverness between these two periods, and much had changed and
stayed the same. I'd been there for a few days conducting interviews across rural and more remote places and was feeling tired at
the end of interviews, often spent in coffee shops, and often being
eyed suspiciously – despite the supposedly protective provisions of
the Equality Act 2010.

The LGBTQ+ cafe where I'd arranged to meet Nneka became
noisy as it moved from late afternoon to early evening, and we
decided to go across the road, to a more recording-friendly venue.
On entering the venue we were both aware of the stares around the
room, which I read as a cross between confusion and fascination as
people tried to work out our relation to one another – as a smaller
white woman in her forties and a taller, mixed-race women in her
twenties. It seemed we were being read as unlikely companions or

customers. Nneka was young and attractive and stood out within a space populated by a middle-aged white crowd, conscious of the 'like racist little jokes, or maybe getting watched in stores, things like that'. In sitting there – across the road from the queer venue – it seemed that we were between multiple versions of Inverness; as residential and touristic, as city-centre and rural, as potentially queer and very straight. And as overwhelmingly white, despite an international tourist population moving through these streets. I could see other people pausing to place Nneka, a mixed-race young woman, wondering, perhaps, where she was *really* from.

Nneka explained that being mixed-race meant that she experienced a lot of racism in school, moving to the Highlands as a child and being 'one of the few minority families in the area'. While Alisha and Asifa lived in cities with large minoritised ethnic populations – and particularly South Asian populations – community presence did not necessarily protect them from institutionalised racism. The overwhelming whiteness of the Highlands had meant a tighter management around fitting-in; Nneka talked about the racism expressed by her dad, who used to insist that Nneka's hair was cut short in a particular way, rather than being allowed to grow out naturally. This management was framed via normative gendered expectations, in his attempts at producing a masculine son rather than something 'too girly', as shaped too by racist ideas of heritage, embodiment, and belonging:[32]

> But my dad noticed when I was younger like how I was with things, and I was a lot more effeminate. I played with like dolls and things, I liked my mum's clothes. … And I used to love when me and my brother, all the time everyone thought we were girls because of our hair. So our dad used to cut our hair and he used to take things off me, and he used to tell us not to act a certain way. But that was a mix of him being racist and a mix of like not wanting me to be too girly. Like he tried to distance us from like our mum and our grandad and our heritage.

Hair and other embodied and material markers became signs of difference, also reflected in Alisha's and Asifa's discussions about dress codes and hair length. In school, Nneka's memories were of her hair being pulled, and of crying all the time ('people would randomly come up and pull my hair and laugh at it like it's a game'). Like Asifa, she didn't really figure out the 'LGBT stuff' until she was older, partly attributing this to the 'very toxic form of Catholic' education where being gay was 'wrong'. After finishing her first enrolment at college, she didn't feel she could leave her town, and with no known way out she felt suicidal ('I was still stuck in this small ignorant town and I didn't see any way out'). Nneka made several suicide attempts and although not 'fully out' at college, she had recently felt she could 'open up with stuff', including her feelings about being queer. Nneka was involved in Afro-Caribbean societies, but had experienced familiar exclusions and mis-fits there too:

> In college I went to like Afro-Caribbean societies to get appreci-
> ation and stuff for myself. But some of the people in my course
> would make fun when I posted photos or stuff. People who I
> thought were my friends would say things like how I looked like
> the white person of the group because of how light skinned I am,
> and that felt horrible.

Even in the white Highlands of Scotland, Nneka was ever-conscious of the global political environment, of her Scottish-Nigerian background, and the varied and consequential backdrops of life and death as ever-present. In Nigeria, Brazil, Ghana, *and* Scotland, rather than Nigeria, Brazil, Ghana, *not* Scotland, bad things continue to happen:

> I know people in the LGBT community that don't know about
> the amount of stuff that are happening to like trans women of
> colour or like people of colour. Which is like a big thing to me.
> Someone I knew actually went to Ghana or Nigeria for like, to
> help people in need, but they didn't know that certain countries
> had like the death penalty for trans people. Or that it's like very,
> very dangerous for trans people, and they only found out when
> they got there .... There's the change in the Gender Recognition
> Act and what people are saying I'm not surprised. Like I'm not
> really surprised by a lot of things or anything bad that happens

... I heard on a documentary about a trans woman in Brazil had her heart cut out while she was alive. I wasn't surprised by that.

Nneka, like Alisha and Asifa, knew the world to be a hostile place – yet much of that hostility and hatred was experienced as everyday and unsurprising rather than exceptional, as Alisha expressed ('Like it's been like this for decades. How do you think I get through every day?'). Continuing global crises and responses – from the Trump era to the Black Lives Matter movement, from the pandemic to the cost-of-living crisis – impact directly and intimately, including in anticipated life expectancy. As a young mixed-race trans pansexual lesbian in the white Highlands of Scotland, Nneka related how structures of racism, sexism, and transphobia – and how the world generally – becomes 'too much after a while':

... like with Trump and everything or like with what's going on in America or big things in like the UK or the world. I feel like right now with everything I'm going through I can't deal with like a lot of the main things. Something I used to keep up with was like the Black Lives Matter movement and the shooting of trans people and Black people, and especially Black trans women of colour. The life expectancy of someone like me being trans in America is thirty-five because of how trans women of colour are treated. I don't know what my like life expectancy in the UK is ... probably a bit higher but not much higher ... I used to keep up with a lot of what was going on in America and any attacks in the UK, but it was just too much after a while.

Nneka's, Alisha's, and Asifa's accounts as working-class lesbians of colour resonate across time and place in their experiences of class-race-gender-sexuality. These materialise as the intersectional conditions of 'real life', through migrancy, displacement, and belonging, and become the 'bread and butter' of everyday life, to use Nneka's words. These everyday realities are played out on the global stage, and through austerity to (post)Brexit pandemic times. Flashpoints across time and place link conservative and neoliberal forces as actively perpetrating intersectional inequalities. Within Nneka's, Alisha's, and Asifa's lives this has been felt in living through the Thatcher years of Section 28, into New Labour's 'war on terrorism' and the ramping up of homonationalist racism, and via the escalation of new-old gender conservativisms. In being 'Rebel Dykes' their experiences are situated empirically in the everyday, with a sense of suspicion towards easy understandings of life getting better ('I still experience racism and sexism and stuff. Just people know how to be more careful about it'—Alisha).

CONCLUSION: POLITICAL CARES

Thinking about bodies out of time and out of place, I've returned to 'the lesbian' then and now – including in my own selection and production of real lesbian lives. Alisha suggested that being more careful individually might not lead to more genuine, trans-formative, collective care practices; the sense of intent – of what is held, carried, and returned to, and for what political purpose – is ever-important. I reread the case of the lesbian and in these empirical accounts are political possibilities, re-imaginings and intersectional solidarities, responsive to the question of 'what's left of queer?'[33] Political cares can collide, including in queer agendas – some battles are amplified and others glossed over, becoming the quiet rather than spectacular scenes of everyday working-class queer life. At the end of *Rebel Dykes* we hear what happened to the people in the film, underscored by absences too, as people didn't survive but suffered and were lost, impacted by the HIV/AIDS crisis, and the wholesale undercutting of the welfare state amidst increasing global conservativism manifest in the Thatcher–Reagan alliance (as in the Johnson–Trump union discussed by Nneka). The question of who will survive these connected crises – and who will be carried in careful returns, repetitions, and redresses – is one which working-class queers still face. Chapter 7, 'Towards a Queer Working-Class Reading List', positions re-reading in and through the changing queer-feminist classroom alongside my own entry points, from being a student to becoming a teacher. This is an ongoing effort, as the struggle in fighting for the queer left always is.

7

Towards a Queer Working-Class Reading List

I am currently taking action short of a strike as part of the University and College Union's (UCU) industrial action to defend our right to a fair pension. Response times will be slower for the duration of the dispute.
    —My out-of-office auto-reply, 2006, 2018, 2019, 2021, 2022 ...

In *Queerly Classed* Susan Raffo[1] asks a series of pointed questions rewritten on this page more than two decades on, as answers are still sought:

- Do you talk about class and class systems as a part of your life? If so, how do you talk about class? If not, why not?
- What determines class location? Money? Family history? Trade and employment? Status? Health? Geography? Race and ethnicity? Ability?
- What do the terms gay community, gay and lesbian community, glbt community, or queer community mean to you? What goes into the making of a community?
- Are these issues queer issues: Immigration? Health care? Social services? Education? Affordable housing? What makes an issue queer?
- How does sexuality play into the economic side of class issues? The cultural side? Do you see a distinction between these things?

These lists are provocative and persistent, measuring what comes to count as class, both economically and culturally, and what is deemed outside, uninteresting, or excessive to the realms of class or

Figure 7.1 'Outwrite Women's Newspaper', Glasgow Women's Library.

Source: author's image.

queer. Interdisciplinary and academic-activist orientations reposition class-queer scholarship and become ways of sorting class lives, as separate from queer lives (including in reading lists, disciplines, and key figures).[2] But the question 'do *you* talk about ...' can pull these *personal* parts together. I talk and read about class and queer a lot. I turn back to reading lists, and reading practices, to think through what circulates and why this matters: what endures when the reading lists are updated, and when we strike out again in our academic productions? This chapter locates rereading in and through the changing queer-feminist classroom, overlapping with my own entry points, from being a student to becoming a teacher.

Figure 7.2 Official picket poster, 2018.
Source: author's image.

In striking for better pay and conditions, as per the ongoing University and College Union's (UCU) strike action across the UK's higher education sector, members are, at least in some ways, arguing for better (feminist) classrooms and improved reading lists, as a means of resourcing knowledge, activism, and change. The out of office auto-reply signifies, in the instance of strike action, uncertainty about the university, and a collective pushback against precarity, sector underfunding, and pension loss. Being 'out of office' conveys an emptiness and an absence, but for a political purpose and presence. Animated by such struggles, Silvia Federici[3] argues that 'coming out is like going on strike', echoed in

Chapter 2 28th Jan 2022
Chapter 5- Queer Provincialisms in Post-Brexit Britain 26 Jan 2022
Chapter 5- Brexit 25 Jan 2022
Chapter 3 Doing Queer Data 14th Jan 2022
Chapter 5- Brexit 24 Jan 2022
Chapter 7 Working Class Lesbian Life 15th Dec. 2021
Chapter 4 Queer Pandemic 18th Jan 2022
Chapter 4 Queer Pandemic 14th Jan 2022
Pandemic is personal cut 17th Jan 2022
Chapter 2 Matt's review 17th Jan 2022
Chapter 3 Doing Queer Data 11th Jan 2022
Chapter 2 12 Jan 2021
Literature review edit_shift 12 Jan 2022
Chapter 1 12 Jan 2021
Chapter 3 Doing Queer Data 10th Jan 2022
Chapter 3 Doing Queer Data 9th Jan 2022
Chapter 3 Doing Queer Data 6th Jan 2022
Chapter 2 30 Dec 2021
Chapter 1 31 Dec 2021
Chapter 1 28 Dec 2021.docx
Chapter 3 Queer-Class Methods 13th Oct. 2021
Chapter 1 24 Dec 2021.docx
Chapter 1 23 Dec 2021.docx
Chapter 1 23 Dec 2021_SG.docx
Chapter 1 22 Dec 2021
Chapter 5- Brexit 9th Nov. 2021.docx
Acknowledgement 19 Dec 2021
Chapter 1 19 Dec 2021
Bibliography Dec 2021
Conclusion 5th Aug 2021
Chapter 2 18 Nov 2021
Chapter 4 Queer Pandemic 1st Oct 2021
Chapter 6 Queer in Austerity 10 Nov. 2021.docx

Figure 7.3   Reading-writing list, 2021–22.
Source: author's image.

the autonomous collective Queer Strike's long-term efforts (previously Wages Due Lesbians). Lesbian struggle prompts and compels anti-capitalist thinking and action, where 'The Dykes Go Marching On' in writing out and outwriting (Figure 7.1). As auto-replies are set up to signpost, and even buffer, industrial action, I think about coming out (again) and how my auto-reply might function as a reading list, a signposting of what persists and connects:

> For radical hope and writing out-side the classroom, go first to bell hooks, to Audre Lorde, to Toni Cade Bambara, to June Jordan …

For radical lesbianism, political lesbianism, the lesbian continuum, lesbians as not-women, go to Andrea Dworkin and Monique Wittig ...

For intersectionality, go to Kimberlé Crenshaw, Floya Anthias, Avtar Brah, and see this in action via the 1977 activist statement of the Combahee River Collective ...

For the 'political economy of sex', see Rosemary Hennessey and Alexandra Chasin ...

To re-connect with #workingclassacademics, go back to Pat Mahony, Christine Zmroczek, Michelle M. Tokarczyk, and link first-generation students then and now...

For readings on class and feminism, find a copy of Bev Skeggs' *Formations of Class and Gender*, compare with Julie Bettie's US-based book *Women Without Class* ...

To border-cross as a reader, read *This Bridge Called My Back: Writings by Radical Women of Colour*, edited by Cherríe Moraga and Gloria Anzaldúa ...

Take instruction from Hazel Carby's *White Women Listen!* ...

To listen and hear beyond the UK–US mapping of queer, see work by Hongwei Bao, Jin Haritaworn, Nkunzi Zandile Nkabinde, Elahe Haschemi Yekani, Ting-Fai Yu ...

On the limits of liberal inclusion, see Lisa Duggan and Wendy Brown's *States of Injury* ...

See Jasbir Puar for a critique of homonationalism ... and for queer of colour critique, continue with Puar and go to back to Cathy Cohen, to José Esteban Muñoz, to Roderick Ferguson (and back to bell hooks, to Audre Lorde) ...

For a class critique of queer theory, see Matt Brim's *Poor Queer Studies* ...

See Anne Balay's *Semi Queer* and *Steel Closets* ethnographies ... continue with stories from working-class queer writers, pick up the substantial *Blue, Too: More Writing By (For or About) Working-Class Queers*, edited by Wendell Ricketts ...

For queer mutual aid, see Dean Spade's *Mutual Aid: Building Solidarity During the Crisis* and read this alongside the *Women in Collective Action* anthology and *Heart of the Race: Black Women's Lives in Britain* by Beverley Bryan, Stella Dadzie, and Suzanne Scafe. Consider the roots of mutual aid groups[4] ... of how to #decolonisingthecurriculm, as the #BlackLivesMatter and #MeToo movements persist and intersect...

Go back to Lisa Mckenzie's *Getting By: Estates, Class and Culture in Austerity Britain* for an understanding of how working-class people have always got by and made do, as back to work, as business as usual ...

Do not go back to business as usual ...[5]

The coming-out-going-on-strike auto-reply lists and interrupts as a presence signalling a broader absence, including queer working-class reading lists as legitimate, recognised, and resourced in feminist classrooms. In 'To(o) Queer the Writer', Anzaldúa writes:

> as a reader, I usually have more in common with the Chicana dyke than I do with the white, middle-class feminist. I am in possession of both ways of reading – Chicana working-class, dyke ways of reading, and white middle-class heterosexual and male ways of reading. I have had more training in reading as a white, middle-class academic than I do reading as a Chicana. Just like we have more training reading as men.[6]

I read, write, and reference as part of the politics of citation as 'epistemic reparation', knowing that I owe a responsibility to past-present-future feminisms.[7] I leave the reading list open in the ellipses and as an instruction to write-out and outwrite other classrooms.

The classroom continues to be a contentious place, with some taking up more space than others.[8] Some push in as new entrants, others exit, and some are claimed as the very signs of a feminist arrival – that the university has taken account of gender and 'EDI issues'. The purpose of a reading list isn't just to appear on the page – as a diversity count turned into evidence of the post-feminist, post-colonial, intersectional classroom. The implied linearity to reading, as accumulated knowledge or identity (being a student, becoming an academic), also sits against a sense of revisions as well as political repetitions. And these occur in a context where to be a queer-feminist academic is to become the 'gender person', limiting readability. Feminist possibilities in and outside of the classroom are themselves subject to change and contestation (as Judith Lorber stated, 'I myself was originally a liberal feminist, then a socialist feminist, and now consider myself to be primarily a social construction feminist, with overtones of postmodernism and queer theory'[9]). Reading lists are updated, but saying you are a radical lesbian, socialist, or queer feminist may send you back to the 1960s, '70s, '80s or '90s ...

Here I reread lesbian, socialist, and queer writings as they move me back into queer-feminist space as a site of queer-left struggle. Such struggle is also carried in striking out again, opening and closing the book, entering and exiting the classroom, and reconfiguring 'real life' struggle. Feminist classrooms and the work in sustaining these – including reading, doing, being, repeating 'feminist' – might always be queer. Feminist classrooms might be 'queer before queer', representing a continuous striking out, and outwriting, against normative lists and counts.[10] Renewed calls for queer-left action, for thinking through 'What's left of queer?' and the possibility of a 'queer materialism', circle back to Raffo's questions, opening this chapter. I move (back) towards a queer working-class reading list, not as exhaustive but as returned to, and ongoing, queer-feminist labour.[11]

THE FEMINIST CLASSROOM: FROM THE BOTTOM READING GROUP TO A ROOM OF HER OWN?

... so you've gone through this working-class school where everybody is pretty rough, into this middle-class environment where everybody's wearing little white gloves and they were handing out books in English class and I got my book and I went 'Sir there's a dirty great hole in my book!' and he just looked at me and went 'Catherine, the whole is neither dirty nor is it great' (laughs). I didn't speak again for the next three years. I just thought 'Right, ok, I've got it now!' ... All through my teens I was a closet case, 'cause I realised I was a lesbian when I was seven or eight or something ... I just thought, with all this other shit going on, I'm not going to announce it, I'm not going to draw attention to myself.

—Cathy, 37, white, lesbian, interviewed 2001

How could I have erased the lesbians?! Thanks for pointing that out!

—Gender Studies student email, 2021

As an academic I have an office. In many respects this is the room of my own, but it is a space which is institutionally structured, including through demarcations of becoming academic. The educational journey which Cathy describes resonates with my own, in terms of getting by and keeping my mouth shut in spaces, from school classrooms to university settings, that reward fluency and instruct the working-class student to 'speak up!' and 'participate!' – often constituting painful shaming processes rather than encouragements. As books are passed around, some are left with a sense that this material is not for us, and that there are costs as well as credentials in learning. Here, I revisit my own navigations of, in, and towards a queer working-class reading list, as one not found at school (and not easily accessed upon entering university).

In trying to get 'left of queer',[12] including going back and moving forward to the queer left, I think about which feminist concepts are reread, appearing and disappearing on the bookshelf. There is hope and possibility in rereading rather than in finalising the reading list. Books open up and shut down possibilities, laying the foundation for what might come afterwards, through closing, returning to, and rewriting their pages:

> Rereading, like caretaking, is an act of repetition. In deconstruction and the queer theory that has emerged from it, repetition is generally understood to be imperfect and its imperfections productive of new and liberating possibilities.[13]

Long-term reading also makes apparent proprietorial claims and losses, of excitement, hope, frustration, and exhaustion, of being stuck on the same page or surpassing it, of closing and opening books, and as entry to and exit from the real world. Still, *The Dykes Go Marching On*! Our readings date and 'out' our academic journeys, and mine has been possible because of persisting queer-feminist writing; this persists as repetition, déjà vu, incompletion, and revision. And it persists as a political possibility striking our senses: 'This work shook me up. Here was writing in which an embodied experience of power provides the basis of knowledge.'[14]

My entry into and persistence in social sciences has been an interdisciplinary one. I've deployed academic categories, lists, and distinctions in claiming a sense of (mis)fit. I've inhabited Women's and Gender Studies as well as mainstream Sociology, and cognate disciplines of Education, Geography, and Social Policy. These institutional (dis)locations allow for long-term reading practices, but they are also differently read through institutional hierarchies, and subject to political shifts inside and outside of higher education. In the early 2000s I started a Gender Studies Masters, before undertaking a PhD at the University of York, which, at the time, housed one of the very few Women and Gender Studies centres in the UK. Starting on this programme meant starting a new reading list – one that productively collided with much mainstream-reading-as-proper-knowledge. I was introduced to feminism in all its waves – and as complication to waves.[15] Before then, feminism had featured as one slightly quirky insertion in an otherwise straight white male reading list; Mary Wollstonecraft in her *A Vindication of the Rights of Woman* (1792) likely still fills this slot in multiple social science degrees. I read this too. As an undergraduate, I learned the essentials of a good reading list – to always include Karl Marx, Émile Durkheim, Max Weber, Erving Goffman, Pierre Bourdieu. I felt ambivalent about these essential readings despite their long-term purchase and prestige, and their knowing and naming of class formations, categories, and processes. These remain required readings, even if radical lesbian texts might tell us just as much about social stigma, distinction, anomie, alienation.[16]

I discovered Gender Studies accidentally, and my accidental academic existence traces back and forward (see Chapter 2). Yet it is no accident that feminist classrooms are ever located as sites of trouble, subject to surprise, hostility, and banning. Queer-feminist classrooms are highly contested because of their transformative potential, underscoring the real-life consequences of reading. My institution restarted a Gender Studies degree programme more than two decades after it was shut down, and these openings and closures are familiar across both the UK and international contexts.[17] These processes circle around feminist labour and the coming and going of institutional support, with pioneering work from past scholars creating enduring legacies, as points of departure and contestation.[18]

Being in the feminist classroom introduced me to US lesbian author Dorothy Allison's body of work, including her memoir *Two or Three Things I Know for Sure* and other powerful stories such as *Trash: Short Stories*, *Bastard Out of Carolina*, and *Skin: Talking About Sex, Class & Literature*, radical in their imagining of other worlds ('Two or three things I know for sure, and one is that I would rather go naked than wear the coat the world has made for me').[19] I read *The Passionate Mistakes and Intricate Corruption of One Girl in America*, alongside *Dykes to Watch Out For* and *Hothead Paisan: Homicidal Lesbian Terrorist*.[20] I read Ann Bannon's *Odd Girl Out* as a bestselling paperback classic of twentieth-century lesbian culture.[21] Yet I couldn't quite shake the feeling of (not) learning and absorbing proper theory or knowledge, as Michelle Tea's books transported me to a Californian landscape, albeit one marked by poverty and the daily fight for survival facing young, homeless queers in 1990s San Francisco. In these readings I got closer to feeling my way through Raffo's opening questions.

I found Bev Skeggs' book *Formations of Class and Gender* in the library and sat down, there and then, in the aisles. I hadn't been introduced to or assigned the book on classroom reading lists, instead finding it accidently as I searched for required 'core readings'. I found the category of 'working-class women' in-between bookshelves and reading lists, as queer, intersectional, and coalitional, resisting disappearance as '... invisible, deconstructed to irrelevance, dismissed as part of a redundant concept, or pathologized as just another "social problem"'.[22] In Gender Studies, I read the work of feminist theorists and activists such as bell hooks' *Teaching to Transgress*; *Feminism is for Everybody*; *Where We Stand: Class Matters*; *Teaching Community: A Pedagogy of Hope*.[23] I read Audre Lorde's defiant self-definition as a 'black, lesbian, mother, warrior, poet', and her words 'Your silence will not protect you'[24] were posted up in the feminist spaces I moved through.

The powerful refrain against silence was felt and followed in hearing histories, presences, and absences, preceding, enabling, and exceeding my own. I read *Zami: A New Spelling of My Name*,[25] about lesbians living in New York and Mexico during the 1950s–1970s, and *Black British Feminism*,[26] both tackling racism and national belonging, as well as questions around sexuality and class, and the possibilities of feminism beyond white, middle-class women. In repeating the new-to-me feminist mantra 'the personal is political', I wondered why the personal hadn't been political or in any way present in past classrooms. In valuing the contested space of Gender Studies, the temptation can be to smooth over gaps in the feminist classroom to pull us all in with a personalised 'arrival' – feminism is us! In this, there are proprietorial as well as political investments.

My initial feminist readings were often introductions – and confrontations – and an appropriate question would be 'why hadn't I come across these texts previously?' And, 'why hadn't I reached for these beyond my own bounded bookends?' My first experience of many feminist readings underscored my own whiteness, as well as the whiteness of and whitewashing within feminism. Ruth Frankenberg's *White Women, Race Matters* positioned whiteness as '... a set of locations that are historically, socially, politically, and culturally' produced, and as a cumulative name assigning 'everyone a place in the relations of racism'.[27] Lorde's biomythography spoke of race, sexuality, class, and gender as the '... materials of our lives',[28] as collectively amassed. In reading *Zami* I was pulled in, seeing how history, biography, and myth could creatively combine and how 'woman' and 'feminism' may themselves be mythical constructs (un)done through material circumstances, coalitions, and solidarities. Class, race, gender, and sexuality were repositioned as mutually constitutive and always in process, rather than as singular entitles or separate struggles, as per Raffo's (1997) nudging questions that opened this chapter. Widely attributed to Kimberlé Crenshaw,[29] the practice of intersectionality as a coalitional politics of solidarity was present in mandates and manifestos, as the '... development of *integrated* analysis and practice based upon the fact that the major systems of oppression are interlocking'.[30]

In the classroom we were asked to think about 'Where We Stand', encompassing methodological debates around feminist standpoint theory, and Black feminist thought.[31] The class nervously giggled at the idea of a 'hierarchy of oppressions', or the 'oppression Olympics', as we nonetheless sought to gauge where and how we'd fare in such measures and counts, grappling with the 'BIG THREE' categories of intersectionality (race, class, gender) and even with '14 lines of difference'.[32] I read personal accounts written by working-class feminist academics as always implicating other lines. Rather than just dwelling on quantitative class measurements as a place in the table, I felt I had a place at the feminist table, even if it was shaky and often upturned. The instruction that '*Class Matters!*', re-told as a common grounding, was absorbing with traces of earlier circulations, including in Charlotte Bunch and Nancy Myron's lesbian-feminist collective volume *Class and Feminism: A Collection of Essays from the Furies*.[33] I read Rita Mae Brown's *The Last Straw* depicting class differences between middle- and working-class lesbians in the USA, alongside Lilian Faderman's *Odd Girls and Twilight Lovers*.[34] I read Carolyn Steedman's *Landscape for a Good Woman* (1986), pulled in by her description of crying in the archives as classed-gendered lives re-materialised. I read Leslie Feinberg's *Stone Butch Blues*[35] about life in 1970s' USA, a 'call to action' and a depiction of lesbian scenes as class divided rather than mixed, also represented in *Left Out: The Politics of Exclusion – Essays 1964–1999*.[36] I read Joan Nestle's *A Restricted Country*,[37] documenting intimate accounts of lesbian, feminist, civil rights movements in the USA. Yet the feminist classroom then, like now, often restricted readings, privileging Global North contexts and re-constituting processes of being 'Left Out'.

My Gender Studies class searched the extensive local collections of Bishopsgate Institute and Hall-Carpenter Archives, documenting the development of queer activism in the UK since the 1950s. The language of Marxist, queer, and anti-colonialist theory was present in archived committee minutes, in queer organising and self-publishing. Archives cast transgressive traces back and forward, as did Jackie Kay's *Trumpet*,[38] causing classroom pauses on identity, embodiment, passing, fitting-in, and outness. Inspired by the life of Billy Tipton, an American jazz musician who lived with the secret of being trans, I read *Trumpet* alongside radical feminist texts. In *Compulsory Heterosexuality and Lesbian Existence*,[39] Adrienne Rich pushed against straight–gay binaries with the idea of the 'lesbian continuum'. Controversially, Rich defined lesbianism not necessarily on the basis of sexuality, but as relational and intimate bonds between women. Rich's 'lesbian continuum' encompassed all women-identified experiences as routine and everyday, thereby countering invisibility, including the difficulty of interpreting distinctly 'lesbian experiences' and events from the past. Again, these possibilities sung out from the Gender Studies classroom, but they didn't always sing out in harmony, with 'political lesbianism' seemingly encompassing everything, yet also desexualising lesbian existence as arguably another heterosexist erasure.[40]

Monique Wittig's statement that lesbians were not women, for 'woman' only has meaning in heterosexual systems of thought, became my go-to gender trouble, as longstanding feminist attempts to abandon, and transform gender.[41] I returned to this phrase as I grappled with Judith Butler's *Gender Trouble: Feminism and the Subversion of Identity* and *Bodies That Matter: On the Discursive Limits of Sex.*[42] The idea of gender as a performative repetition, legitimising social hierarchies in its continual patterned enactment, still causes much gender trouble. It still causes pause on the longstanding question of 'woman' and 'woman-hood' as categories which feminism invests in and responds to, but which are also subject to questioning, revisioning, and destabilisation. Identity as a 'category error' both appealed to and troubled me as I thought about how categories constrained – as well as enabled – identifications and possibilities, always exceeding attempts to finalise, via sample-sizes, list-counts, or the 'awkward etc'. Butler focused instead on the possibilities of the 'embarrassing etc', and how the list of identifications, classifications, experiences is always incomplete:

> ... theories of feminist identity ... Of color, sexuality, ethnicity, class, and able-bodiedness invariably close with an embarrassed 'etc.' at the end of the list. Through this horizontal trajectory of adjectives, these positions strive to encompass a situated subject, but invariably fail to be complete. This failure, however, is instructive: what political impetus is to be derived from the exasperated 'etc.' that so often occurs at the end of such lines?[43]

I grappled with a sense of wanting all possibilities, while wary of what I might be misreading, or producing as an 'etc'. I read and reread Butler's ('Merely Cultural') exchange with Nancy Fraser ('Heterosexism, Misrecognition and Capitalism: A Response to Judith Butler') on socialist feminism, and the enduring legacy of Marxism.[44] I understood that Butler and Fraser disagreed on how capitalism and heterosexism are linked: Fraser located certain oppressions as part of the political economy, whilst relegating others – including struggles for LGBTQ+ rights – to the cultural sphere. In contrast, Butler argued for an expansive conceptualisation of materiality, including the reproduction of genders, sexualities, and the heterosexual nuclear family. I understood that capitalism and heterosexism were linked; I also drew lines around readings on the 'political economy of sex' and 'performative significations', around queer theory and materialist feminist analysis, around empirical weight and theoretical abstraction, while wanting to also hold these playfully as well as politically.

The idea of gender becoming 'nothing other than the effects of drag' has been criticised for exceptionalising trans people as performative queer icons seemingly far removed from real-life oppression. Troubling the assumed fixity of sex-gender-sexuality, trans scholarship has necessarily complicated the category of 'woman' over again.[45] But rather than just 'serving as figures for a kind of anti-binary subversion of gender',[46] trans realities and politics return to intersectional issues, including class and race. Drawing on Jules Gill-Peterson, David L. Eng and Jasbir K. Puar note: '... trans politics can also produce essentialised identities ... calling out of cisgender identity without sufficient recognition of its racial valences, its proprietary weight, middle class privileges, or its relation to histories and futures of racial capitalism'.[47]

In attending to trans liveability within capitalist, racist, and cis-het structures, as well as the differences within cis gender identities and realities, these words echo across the feminist classrooms I've moved through. Contemporary calls resonate with Cohen's calling out in the 1990s of queer activism and scholarship for privileging certain forms of (gay, male, white) queerness to the exclusion of 'other queers', including straight-queers as heterosexuals outside of heteronormativity (for example Black single mothers on welfare).[48] The possibilities and limitations of feminist-queer classrooms are subject to re-interrogation, including when an utterance of 'queer' and/or 'trans' may have educational and career jeopardising effects.[49] These readings, criticisms, and re-directions blur and return to imagined starting points, to questions of the scope and possibilities of feminist solidarities and, to use Sara Ahmed's words, I would also suggest '… that it is transfeminism today that most recalls the militant spirit of lesbian feminism in part because of the insistence that crafting a life is political work'.[50]

In reading in and out of time, through initial and extended classroom encounters, I've moved between hyphenated queer-feminist frames. Ahmed notes that lesbians 'over-inherit' queerness, sometimes positioned as a 'step in a queer direction', as pre-queer, including in the narration of disciplinary feminist-to-queer studies, whilst also becoming an embodied social signifier of the past to be disavowed. In contemporary times, 'lesbian' has been mobilised by right-wing, conservative and TERF agendas. Such a move effaces radical legacies within lesbian activisms, politics, and theorising, as lesbian, feminist, trans-inclusive, and queer.[51] Re-essentialising identities acts against intersectional solidarities and limits feminism to a certain kind of 'woman', a criticism stretching back to the much-cited nineteenth-century statement by Sojourner Truth, 'Ain't I a Woman?'[52]

Despite synergies and repetitions, the relationship between queer theory and intersectionality is complicated. Queer-of-colour critique, research on queer diasporas, queer disability scholarship, transgender studies, and queer and class analysis stretch the listing of the big three social divisions ('race, class, gender') as an 'intersectional mantra'. In considering if 'queer comes to mean simply affluent white gay men?' José Esteban Muñoz[53] proposed 'dis-identification' as a tactic to work against normative (white, middle-class, cisgendered) queer theory. The go-tos of queer theory – and class theory – can also be dis-identified with, where Raffo's opening provocations may return us to the 'queer ordinary'.[54] But while the production of a singular reading list can be queered, whiteness still pervades the feminist classroom. Jennifer Nash highlights how intersectionality has been celebrated as Black Feminism's primary intellectual and political contribution to feminist theory, evoking anxious as well as hopeful feelings: citation can allow white feminists to feel that intersectionality has been *done*. Through gender studies teaching, white feminists claim and move on through Black feminists' labour and legacies. Nash then asks what happens when intersectionality as a term becomes '... popularized, institutionalized, ossified ...', and when usage by white feminists stands in for diversity or inclusiveness, rather than as a reminder of ongoing racist exclusion: 'women of color remain eminently useful to the progress narrative Women's Studies wishes to create for itself, where the fullness of women of color's arrival within Women's Studies is always "about to be"'.[55]

In describing my personal readings through Gender Studies I'm aware of my own academic journeying and selection – of what made it on to my remembered reading lists and how my readings place me (including as a good or bad selector, reader, or feminist). In reading my way through feminisms, I mean not to entirely absorb, finalise, or own it. Feminism is necessarily an interrupted project, persisting through its own interruptions.[56] Locating queer-feminist conversations as hyphenated and ongoing can mean fighting again for the queer left, where provocations are both pointed and circular in moving towards a queer working-class reading list.

> I was thinking the other day, it was Lesbian Visibility Week. I get asked quite a lot 'who are your heroes?' You know, lesbian heroes kind of thing ... I'm not, you know, I'm not like 'oh this famous lesbian is the person I admire'. Because I think the thing that I've always found most inspiring are actually working-class lesbians who are just getting on with being themselves in not always the most easy circumstances.
> —Senior Manager in a UK LGBTQ organisation

QUEER CLASSROOMS

Word Search: QUEER

queer-feminist classrooms
DO THEY EXIST, QUEERLY
queer left

IS NOT AT THE TABLE
queer theory
LEAVES OFF
To be sure, queer
BEING QUEER
A New Queer Agenda
UNCERTAINTIES
'queer'
NEW! QUEER! AGENDA!
queer connections
'SCARE QUOTES'
radical queer shifts
INSIDE-OUTSIDE
Queer of colour scholarship
DIS-IDENTIFICATIONS
whiteness of queer lives
BLACK FEMINISM
queer as a discipline
WHITE UNIVERSTIES
'What's Left Of Queer?'
INTERDISCIPLINE
Queer-Marxism
GO LEFT, LEFT AGAIN
working-class queers
CIS-HETEROPATRIACHY
Rich Queer Studies
'REAL LIFE'
Queer precariat
WHO LIVES HERE?
Poor queers
WHO WORKS HERE?
Semi-queer
WHO IS HERE?
                —From Who's Here? Who's Queer? workshop, 2022

The above word search of sorts – listed in looking back through
a piece of my own writing (this chapter) – was made and rather
awkwardly shared in the Who's Here? Who's Queer? workshop

(2022).[57] The key-queer words became a search back and forward, and a rewrite of this chapter section where I had been trying to summarise the move to or difference between the feminist class-room and the queer classroom. My pre- and likely post-workshop stalls came from not quite believing the divide – or timeline – I was constructing, of feminist times 'then' versus queer times 'now'. Queer maybe functions best as a provocation and, like feminism, perhaps one which is always failing, or failed by, incorporation into state or institutional structures (The Classroom).

In the feminist classroom of the 1990s and 2000s I read in detail about feminist waves and branches – of liberal, socialist, radical, lesbian, Black, trans feminisms – moving through and being convinced in turn of the worth of each. In turn, feminisms failed inside and outside of the classroom as life continued in non-feminist ways. Despite these stalls, felt both personally and politically, feminism can and likely should crash into the classroom as a disruptive, discomforting force. In being introduced to queer theory in the early 2000s I felt the subversive potential of the classroom. But I also felt that *I* might not quite be the subversive presence or force imagined within Queer Theory, thus beginning a longstanding concern with the 'outness of queer'.[58] In Who's Here? Who's Queer? I asked about who is *still* here? Who was *never* here? Who might yet be here?

Feminism has allowed for and supported different entry points to, with, and through the classroom – Twitter becomes a digital classroom of sorts, re-circulating feminist words in the wake of bell hooks' death in 2021:[59]

> The academy is not paradise. But learning is a place where paradise can be created. The classroom, with all its limitations, remains a location of possibility. In that field of possibility we have the opportunity to labour for freedom … to transgress.

Where feminism has often started with and stretched ideas of lived experience, queer theory quite often felt too hard and too abstract. In feeling this way, I was, and still am, conscious of misreading and missing the mark in knowing, citing, and even potentially being queer/academic. Even as queer connects back to feminist keywords it generates its own selections, categories, preferences, and patterns, and its own go-to reading list. As someone placed in the 'bottom reading group' at school, feminism had given me a politicised vocabulary through which to locate this, my experience, in relation to other structures. And, acknowledging my own proprietorial claims, the categories of 'class', 'gender', and 'sexuality' felt like 'mine' in these moments too. I now caveat and add 'feminist' or/and 'queer' or/and 'lesbian' or/and 'interdisciplinary' to variously (de)legitimised classroom appearances. I wonder about the academic without caveat or queerness, who doesn't need to do a word search, or search for words …

When the classroom has felt like a penalty it can be difficult to subversively reclaim it, to move out of the corner you've been put in (see Chapter 2). Sometimes queer has felt like a celebration of being in the corner, and these corners and celebrations can, of course, be classed. Rather than abandoning feminism and replacing this with queer, classrooms can function in reconnecting backwards-forwards, between students and teachers and in and out of offices. The workshop, as classroom, offered me that fleeting reconnection, filtered through a one-day event, but as part of a queer persistence through long-term difficulties. At times I felt dated. I felt dated in 'being there' in whatever cycle of the feminist waves might be attributed to the late 1990s or 2000s. Conversely, I felt proudly present in locating myself in a Gender Studies classroom at a time when queer theory felt brand new: a brand which has since become institutionalised and embedded in academia, especially in North America.

Queer theory is often situated as a turning point with and against feminist-LGBT+ scholarship, institutionalised in a range of lesbian and gay, as well as Women's and Gender Studies, programmes from the 1990s. There can be something quite head-turning in still being The Lesbian in the workshop in 2022, even with all the abstractions and anti-categorical articulations. I hold feminism and queer together, as hyphenated, where one cannot be easily separated from the other, as a continuous endeavour rather than as classroom capture or completion. Still, I wondered about the queer presences and absences in our classroom creations, labours, and rewrites.

To be sure (see Word Search: Queer), queer theorising has its own elisions and erasures. In 2000, Rosemary Hennessy highlighted synergies between queer and Marxist approaches, where '... the success of bourgeois patriarchy has relied on ideologies that harness desire and labour according to the injunctions of a heterosexual social order'.[60] In *A New Queer Agenda*,[61] Lisa Duggan and Richard Kim (2012) asked how socioeconomic justice has not yet come to be identified as an LGBTQ+ issue, with Jacob DeFilippis similarly pointing to a 'surreal, stony silence' about the economic crisis.[62] In the queer workshop, I tried to explain my own encounters with the 'bourgeois patriarchy', speaking too of working-class queerness as both a pull back from and a way through academic work. Competing claims of the (in)authenticity of what you were (working-class) and what you are now assumed to be (middle-class) by virtue of becoming a (queer-feminist-lesbian) professor persisted. I felt somewhat straightened out, as if I'd opted out (by opting into academia). Struggling with respective and competing entitlements, the queer-feminist classroom can still be competitive and hierarchical, with academia derided as not 'real life' – what of the real life of a queer academic from a working-class background?

Such questions have a long history, preceding, shaping, and contesting queer theory and activism, including inside *and* outside of academia, as discussed by Cathy Cohen in *Punks, Bulldaggers and Welfare Queens*. Arguing that an understanding of power within queer activism and politics is needed to bridge rather than reinforce the divide between queer and straight lives, Cohen states that:

> Only by recognizing the link between the ideological, social, political, and economic marginalization of punks, bulldaggers, and welfare queens can we begin to develop political analyses and political strategies effective in confronting the linked yet varied sites of power in this country.[63]

In the workshop I told the following fictionalised fact as a fractured real-life account. The queer subject here is one not normally positioned as such – a pregnant, heterosexual, cis woman. And yet her queer body still rarely has a place at the table:

A young lecturer – with a still frequent emphasis on the young – receives an email from her PhD student: the student is going to have a baby, she knows this is a shock, she hopes it won't affect opinions of her or her commitment to work, she questions if this will be recognised, if her funding will continue, her deadline extended, her employability ended ... She wonders if her potential is already being recast as a failure and the sense of being in the wrong time (too young to mother, too young to be a successful academic) is transmitted in these exchanges ...

Work is done in reading between the lines of emails, policies, and funding guidance which speak of equal opportunities, a commitment to diversity, an 'investors in people' status: forms are completed, procedures are followed, and pregnancy is declared at the appropriate time – being 'pregnant enough' (for recognition, extension, advice) is stated as 22 weeks, the official time when institutional recognition can begin. 'You're not the first person to have a baby' is the relayed response to the student's concerns and questions.

The phone rings in the young lecturer's office in response to an advertised research associate vacancy. The potential candidate is ringing to ask if she's still eligible to apply as she's just found out that she is pregnant. The lecturer is thinking equal opps, she's thinking HR. And she's thinking project deadlines. What would you be thinking? Her research associate gives birth, takes time out. She's not entitled to institutional benefits, having not served enough time.

—'Maternity Leave: A Queer Encounter'

There are dis-locations in being and doing queer in academia – including beyond the discrete liberal subject of inclusion discourses and policies. Liberal rights – as entitlements to work, HR protections, and contracts – may still mean that certain workers have to pick up the phone, answer the email, be *in* and *out* of the office ... The desire for transformational coalition politics among those who don't fit in echoes calls for fuller queer connections, explicitly linking to the Black (lesbian) feminism of the Combahee River Collective, Audre Lorde, and Kimberlé Crenshaw. Such 'radical intersectional left analysis' is being rediscovered and put to use in queer-feminist classrooms, with intersectionality return-ing as an explicitly non-identitarian approach in queer-of-colour scholarship:

[Q]ueer of color analysis presumes that liberal ideology occludes the intersecting saliency of race, gender, sexuality, and class in forming social practices. Approaching ideologies of transparency as formations that have worked to conceal those intersections means that queer of color analysis has to debunk the idea that race, class, gender, and sexuality are discrete forma-tions, apparently insulated from one another.[64]

Queer-of-colour scholarship points to the limits of liberal inclu-sion through formal recognition, including in educational settings. Here the mainstreaming of queer programmes sits in contradiction to its own subversive intentions. As with Black feminist scholar-ship there can be a smoothing out of differences that matter, as the outside is occupied, as lines of difference are redrawn, and as categories become relativised as just another difference – if not present or included in the queer-classroom the instruction can be to go *elsewhere*, to the Black Studies programme, or to the working-class university.[65] Sometimes these differences become connecting points and disruptions, with 'mindblowing' effects. In the workshop I used the following illustrative quote to connect Quinn's experience, with mine, with theirs, with ours:

It all very much links in, and it links into like racism and colo-nialism, and it links into ableism and the treatment of disabled people … the treatment of the elderly, the treatment of the very young. Like it's all connected, and feminism as well is the other big one. It's what frustrates me so much about the kind of trans-exclusive radical feminists, is that feminism and trans rights, or LGBT rights even, are so interlinked. And it's the same force that you're fighting against but you've just kind of, you're looking in the wrong place for it. And yeah like the amount of sort of work you could do if you kind of pooled that resource together rather than using it on infighting or kind of going with

kind of the oppressor against someone who's already facing so much like difficulty and oppression. It blows my mind (laughs).
—Quinn, 23, white, gay, non-binary, interviewed 2021

As a graduate involved in LGBTQ+ activism through student societies, Quinn connects intersectional issues to their reimagining of queer politics, as a place of collective struggle and pooled resources, where no one is left off the agenda. Whereas Quinn, like other interviewees, may not phrase the question as 'what's left of queer?'[66] they are nonetheless very much dwelling on the political landscape and the enduring struggle for social justice re-emerging in new-old battles. These issues move in and out of feminist-queer classrooms as our 'real-life'. But often interviewees – as working-class queers – were exactly what and who had been left off queer; on the page, in the classroom, on the reading list.

These questions were repeated in the 2022 workshop, by early-career and established academics, all variously taking up space – some as expectant, some as entitled, and others as accidental academics. These personal positions intersect with broader regimes enacted by the state and in and through the (non-feminist, non-queer) university.[67] In many well-intentioned classrooms, feminist-queer do-gooding can frustrate rather than illuminate, naming inequalities whilst not undoing their pervasive presence: our lives become someone else's list or reading materials. Naming or listing might even be a way to seemingly undo middle-classness or whiteness, to show it as open and attentive (and as classroom talk turns to 'micro-aggressions', we talk about how we can be trained as individuals not to do this). Classroom assertions and insertions come in mainstreamed calls to diversify classrooms, to invite-in the outside. In hearing these calls again – as praise or as blame – queer feelings persist.

Moves to include can occlude, and inviting in the right subject at the right time can also signal a capital, even a queer capital. In the Zoom chat, someone asked us to think about diversifying the choice of invited speakers – we were instructed to think across intersectional 'protected characteristics', and the Equality Act 2010 is recited as a good measure. On (not) being visibly representative of enough diversity (as invited speaker), I think about who ever can be, as political-personal pains reframe these queer questions. The event arguably pitched as a counter to straight and queer normativity, yet here again queer problems arise – 'local academics' were invested with value and authenticity as a likely counter to the elsewhere of often-US-based queer-celebrity-academia. The academic from Glasgow might take up that space and might even posture towards being more real than others. But claims to authenticity are gendered, racialised, and classed even in 'wee', 'provincial' places, where the local has a currency, performed against the global as elite (Chapter 4). The move to extend or go elsewhere or otherwise might mean in practice that you are invited in because someone else is overbooked (you might even be told this!): you fill the space but don't fit the space. The recuperation or use of the local by the elite university can be a moment of changing or confirming 'who's here, who's queer' as a declarative identity statement, or as a persistent questioning. I upload my readings to the Zoom chat. I feel out-of-date. I feel local.

I've dis-identified from the queer classroom in my movements backwards-forward, and as hyphenation or bridge between queer-feminism. In the workshop – like all the workshopping in and across academia – I wonder if my words are too harsh. 'That was very thought provoking' come the replies – with few claps or smiles or party emojis as feedback. As part of my local Glasgow-based queer academic talk, I wanted to trouble the terms used in inviting and advertising: I asked participants to think about what might be held in common between locations and stories, and what resonates across the page, with their own experiences. I brought up the example of Will as making a claim to being an intersectional subject, or an 'intersectional I':

> I would say anyone perusing my Twitter feed would probably realise it's sexuality and LGBT+ inclusion … I would hope people would perceive me as intersectional, that it's about human rights. So I think, we have Black Lives Matter, there's disability rights, there's LGBT+ rights, there's age rights. Yes, and each of these things are incredibly important. I think it's so important that it's just, it's human, it's people, so just accept them for who they are.
> —Will, 35, white, gay, cis man, interviewed 2019

I troubled this claim, troubled intersectionality, troubled queer, and troubled feminism. But in all the trouble, participants were perhaps left wondering how to identify in contemporary higher education, and in the classrooms of today. Trouble becomes potentially easy currency for the queerly credentialised and salaried academic. And yet how do we come to terms with academia including the queer terms produced with, by, and for queer academics? Often these terms are ones of identity, of being rather than doing. Queering as a practice stretches the always incomplete, perhaps always failed LGBTQ+ acronym, or the failed feminist project, as one which always compels our return and revisioning. *Doing* queer-feminism, rather than simply *being* a queer feminist, involves the hard

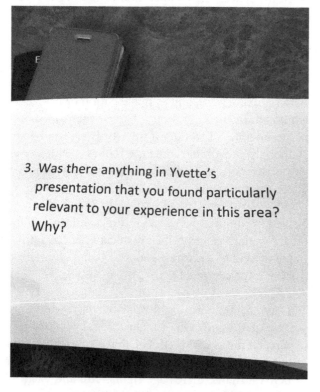

Figure 7.4 Creating Feminist Classrooms feedback prompt, 2001–21.

Source: author's image.

work of production, and reproduction, being done over the long-term, including in classroom commitments. Which is to say, the talk on how to get a job in academia was, and is always, received much more positively than my own.

Over again, I bristle when hearing academic entitlements articulated by what I read as enabled, middle-class queers who, seemingly for the first time, are experiencing some sense of 'educational failure' in not (immediately) getting the academic job they anticipated. I see them seeing me, with my 'professorial privilege', I hear that phrase and I bristle again. Queer questions or call-outs can be classed. In his critique of 'rich queer studies', Matt Brim argues that queer theory seems radical only when the class-base of its production and dissemination is ignored: 'Class is barely indexed in most Queer Studies scholarship. I mean this literally; one only need look at the index of the books on the queer shelf ... Where class appears centrally, queer often does a disappearing act.' Speaking of the respective disappearing acts from queer and class studies, Brim summarises that '... when Queer Studies competes with working-class studies for work space, working-class queers and theories of queer work fall out of focus and get lost'.[68] Despite the potential for a coalitional *and*, these are often separated as oppositional *ors*, including a sense of *my career* or *yours*.

Our classrooms – and our careers – have existed online throughout COVID-19 restrictions and lockdowns. Teachers and administrators have been tasked with making 'reasonable adjustments' in and through classrooms. (Queer) cares are adjusted here too. I think of makeshift offices, of the computer balanced precariously, and the emotional labour of managing classrooms and colleagues when cameras are off and microphones are muted – are we here? Are we queer? I watch and wonder as administrative staff jump in a taxi to literally furnish an academic's home office with equipment during a pandemic ... I think about all the efforts in getting into the classroom to be present as a student and a teacher, and all the ways in which our presence might be rendered absent, as excessive, or not enough, to be adjusted. In the workshop we're shown an exercise in cutting up and shaking out our keywords, and in doing this, things fall to the bottom. This fall-out is less than accidental. And sometimes queer presence and persistence in the

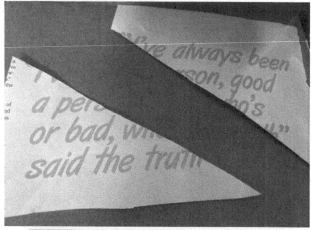

Figure 7.5 and Figure 7.6 From Who's Here? Who's Queer? workshop, 2022, 'My queer box' and 'Resources'.

Source: author's images.

Figure 7.7 and Figure 7.8   From 'Early-Career Researchers' workshop, 2012, 'Back to Square 1?' and 'The PhD wall'.

Source: author's images.

classroom is more routine and mundane, rather than existing as keynote or keywords (or keynote as keyword).

I cycle back through my own workshop organisation and participation, where one of my ex-students talked about going back to square one, in being unemployed post-PhD. These continuous queer-feminist concerns generate resources, as returned to and revitalised reading, as well as stalls and walls. The foundation – or carpet – in my own queer box is a reading list, a review of good feminist reads (see above). I tear off the magazine page which reviews Alison Bechdel's *The Secret to Superhuman Strength* (I spend a good five minutes pausing on the other side, an advert for butch lesbian clothes, wondering whether this should be the underside of my box ...). *Free To Be Me: Refugees' Stories from The Lesbian Immigration Support Group* also appears on the pages, alongside *Duck Feet*, and I nod to my bookshelf with some satisfaction that the real copies are there too, having been turned over page by page.[69] Local-global circuits are felt through these pages: each book deals differently with the borders of community, identity, belonging, and language – with *Duck Feet* written in Scots and with Jane Traies editing in (and out) translated voices which often go unheard. I paste on a message about language: 'Young people instigate new ways of using language. New words and new meanings to words arise all the time. When you are doing your research, pay attention to language and how young people use it.'

I think about queer as identity, as sitting within the LGBTQ+ acronym, while contesting all letters, categories, and identities. I think about the political value of these letters, as placeholders and as energising or tiring – looking to the young people becomes instructive of the future (and who is not in it), and I press a watchful stick-on eye near this cut-out instruction, mindful of my own generational location. In constructing outside the box, we pragmatically make do with the resources we have, while others draw upon their own craft boxes and other objects, often standing in for deconstructed body parts. The walls of my box are papered with a table with an instruction to find a place at it, but there's a brush in the corner, ready to sweep the queer fragments off the page. I get frustrated when my stick-on-eyes won't stick on, and in seeing, or not seeing, the truth, I cut through 'I've always been a person, good or bad, who's said the truth'. That's not the truth of the queer-feminist classroom in challenging and unsettling ideas of objectivity and universalisms.

And yet there is a sense that some productions are better than others. In using shared space, the breakout room and the Jamboard, we visualise, display, and enact our collective efforts ('this is everyone's creation!'), but we also point out 'ours', the box we laboured over, invested in, and created ('that's mine!'). Often the resources we have are under-threat, and even in virtual, potentially more accessible, classrooms, presence and effort are required: queer classrooms still require planning, support, resources, reports. Our workshop required bodies to do the work and to post the package. I retrieve my package – a queer box in the making – from the central post office, sanitising my hands, pulling my face mask up. I'm passed my obviously queer, rainbow-adorned, queer-classroom box by a postie raising an eye, giving a smirk. I let it go as I think about our respective statuses, as key workers or not, and as resourced by key words, or not.

Berlant and Warner point out that queer theory is 'not the theory *of* anything in particular, and has no precise bibliographic shape'.[70] But in making space through our classrooms, in our reading lists, in doing rather than just being queer, we attend to the materiality of presence and absence, and the ever-present fact of 'real life' far from the (queer) classroom.

Butler-Rees, A. and Robinson, N. (2020) 'Encountering precarity, uncertainty and everyday anxiety as part of the postgraduate research journey'. *Emotion, Space and Society*, 37 100743.

Pearce, R. (2020) 'A Methodology for the Marginalised: Surviving Oppression and Traumatic Fieldwork in the Neoliberal Academy'. *Sociology*, 54 (4): 806–24.

Rao, N., Hosein, A. and Raaper, R. (2021) 'Doctoral students navigating the borderlands of academic teaching in an era of precarity'. *Teaching in Higher Education*, 26 (3): 454–70.

Slater, J. and Liddiard, K. (2018) 'Why Disability Studies Scholars Must Challenge Transmisogyny and Transphobia'. *Canadian Journal of Disability Studies*, 7 (2): 83–93.

Taylor, Y. (2016) 'Making space at the (queer) academic table?' In: Crowhurst, I., Santos, C. and King, A. (eds) *Sexualities Research: Critical interjections, diverse methodologies and practical applications*. London: Routledge: 29–40.

Vincent, B., Erikainen, S. and Pearce, R. (2020) *TERF Wars: Feminism and the fight for transgender futures*. London: Sage.
—Who's Here? Who's Queer? reading list

The above resources and readings, as part of an ongoing queer-feminist reading list, reroute us back to Raffo's questions at the beginning of this chapter: 'are these issues queer issues?' 'Are these issues classed?' In the workshop, a speaker talked about the literal 'mess' beyond her computer screen, where online (and offline) classroom presences sometimes hide or literally screen out this real, lived-in background. Urging us to be more public in what lies

Figure 7.9   Queer bookends, 2022.

Source: author's image.

behind academic presences, the speaker highlighted the messier stories, turning the camera in and out. The personal is political, again, still. At the same time, I receive a text message from a friend undertaking a PhD and attending an Academic Futures workshop: 'It was brutal. At the start 60% wanted to pursue an academic career. By the end it was 27% and the missing 33% were crying in the toilets.' Her count may be wrong. But I think again about classrooms as entries and exits, as queer bookends which can reveal the mess, interruption, and labour behind the scenes – with our workloads squeezed and pressed underneath (see my workload calculation underneath the reading list).

The queer-feminist classrooms that I've moved through have highlighted the necessity and difficulty of moving towards a queer working-class reading list. The queer-feminist classroom can be seen as a generative space where readings are continuously done, enlivened, and activated. Such lively learning contexts don't just exist within (higher education) classrooms, occurring and repeating across LGBTQ+ community organisations, individuals, activisms, and in the queer anachronisms of the Queer Left.

Appendix: Texts Referred to in the Auto-Reply Reading List

On radical hope:
hooks, b. (1994) *Teaching to Transgress: Education as the Practice of Freedom*. New York: Routledge; hooks, b. (2000) *Feminism is for Everybody*. London: Pluto; hooks, b. (2000) *Where We Stand: Class Matters*. New York: Routledge; hooks, b. (2003) *Teaching Community: A Pedagogy of Hope*. New York: Routledge; Lorde, A. (1982) *Zami: A New Spelling of My Name*. Massachusetts: Persephone Press; Lorde, A. (1984) *Sister Outsider: Essays and Speeches*. New York: The Crossing Press; Bambara, T.C. (ed.) *The Black Woman: An Anthology*. New York: New American Library; Bambara, T.C. (1981) 'Foreword' in *This Bridge Called My Back*. Persephone Press; Duggan, L. and Muñoz, J. (2009) 'On Hope and Hopelessness: A Dialogue', *Women and Performance* 19: 2.

On political lesbianism:
Dworkin, A. (1980) 'Compulsory Heterosexuality and Lesbian Existence', *Signs*, 5(4): 631–60; Wittig, M. (1992) *The Straight Mind and Other Essays*. Boston: Beacon.

On intersectionality:
Crenshaw, K.W. (1995) 'Mapping the Margins: Intersectionality, Identity Politics, and Violence Against Women of Color' in Crenshaw, K., Gotanda, N., Peller, G., and Thomas, K. (eds) *Critical Race Theory: The Key Writings that Formed the Movement*. New York, NY: New Press, pp. 357–83; Anthias, F. (ed) (1997) *Thinking about Social Divisions: Debates on Class, Gender, Nation and Race*. London: Greenwich University Press; Brah, A. (1996) *Cartographies of Diaspora: Contesting Identities*. London: Routledge.

On sexuality and capitalism:
Hennessy, R. (2000) *Profit and Pleasure: Sexual Identities in Late Capitalism.* New York: Routledge; Chasin, A. (2001) *Selling Out. The Lesbian and Gay Movement Goes to Market.* London: Palgrave.

On working-class academics:
Mahony, P. and Zmroczek, C. (1997) *Class Matters. 'Working Class' Women's Perspectives on Social Class.* London: Routledge; Tokarczyk, M. and Fay, E.A. (1993) *Working-Class Women in the Academy: Labourers in the Knowledge Factory.* Amherst: University of Massachusetts Press; Mckenzie, L. (2015) *Getting By: Estates, Class and Culture in Austerity Britain.* Bristol: Policy Press.

On class and feminism:
Skeggs, B. (1997) *Formations of Class and Gender: Becoming Respectable.* London: Sage; Bettie, J. (2003) *Women without Class: Girls, Race, and Identity.* Berkeley: University of California Press.

On race, ethnicity and migration:
Moraga, C. and Anzaldúa, G. (1984) *This Bridge Called My Back: Radical Writings by Women of Color.* Kitchen Table Women of Color Press; Carby, H. (1982) 'White Woman Listen! Black Feminism and the Boundaries of Sisterhood', *The Empire Strikes Back: Race and Racism in Seventies Britain.* London: Hutchinson, pp. 212–35.

On global queers:
Bao, H. (2020) *Queer China: Lesbian and Gay Literature and Visual Culture under Postsocialism.* London: Routledge; Haritaworn, J. (2015) *Queer Lovers and Hateful Others: Regenerating Violent Times and Places,* London: Pluto; Haschemi Yekanie, E., Michaelis, B., and Dietze G. (2010) '"Try Again. Fail Again. Fail Better": Queer Interdependencies as Corrective Methodologies' in Taylor, Y., Hines, S., and Casey, M. *Theorizing Intersectionality and Sexuality.* Basingstoke: Palgrave, pp. 78–98; Yu, Ting-Fai (2020) 'Reconfiguring Queer Asia as Disjunctive Modernities: Notes on the Subjective Production of Working-Class Gay Men in Hong Kong', *Journal of Homosexuality* 67(6): 863–84.

On the limits of the state and homonationalism:

Duggan, L. (2003) *The Twilight of Equality? Neoliberalism, Cultural Politics, and the Attack on Democracy.* Boston: Beacon Press; Duggan, L. and Richard, K. (2012), 'Preface: A New Queer Agenda', *S&F Online* 10(1–2) (http://sfonline.barnard.edu/a-new-queer-agenda/preface/ [accessed 1 May 2018]; Duggan, L. and Hunter, N. (1995) *Sex Wars: Sexual Dissent and Political Culture.* New York: Routledge; Brown, W. (1995) *States of Injury. Power and Freedom in Late Modernity.* Princeton: Princeton University Press; Cohen, C.J. (1997) 'Punks, Bulldaggers and Welfare Queens. The Radical Potential of Politics' GLQ, 3: 437–65; Muñoz, J.E. (2009) *Cruising Utopia. The Then and There of Queer Futurity.* New York: New York University Press; Ferguson, R. (2004) *Aberrations in Black: Toward a Queer of Color Critique.* Minneapolis: University of Minnesota Press.

On working-class queers:

Brim, M. (2020) *Poor Queer Studies.* Durham, NC: Duke University Press; Taylor, Y., Brim, M., and Mahn, C. (eds) *Queer Precarities in and out of Higher Education.* Bloomsbury; Balay, A. (2018) *Semi Queer. Inside the World of Gay, Trans, and Black Truck Drivers.* Chapel Hill: The University of North Carolina Press; Ricketts, W. (2014) *Blue, Too. More Writing By (for or about) Working-Class Queers.* US: Fourcats Press.

On mutual aid:

Spade, D. (2020) *Mutual Aid: Building Solidarity During the Crisis.* New York: Verso; Sitrin, M. and Colectiva Sembra (2020) *Pandemic Solidarity. Mutual Aid during the Covid-19 Crisis.* London: Pluto; Bryan, B., Dadzie, S., and Scafe, S. (2018) *Heart of the Race. Black Women's Lives in Britain* London: Verso.

Notes

CHAPTER 1

1. hooks, b. (1994) *Teaching to Transgress: Education as the Practice of Freedom*. New York: Routledge.
2. Invoking categories of sexuality, gender, and class continues to be contested, across and between academic spaces. I use 'LGBTQ+' as an umbrella term corresponding to interviewees' own identifications across different fieldwork periods. I have used other terms such as 'LGBT' when used in the original literature, including policy usage (see https://www.stonewall.org. uk/help-advice/faqs-and-glossary/list-lgbtq-terms [accessed 17 October 2021]). Two projects reported on here – 'Working-Class Lesbian Life' and 'Lesbian and Gay Parenting' – retain the more specific terms utilised – and contended – by those projects and participants. Identifications are not static and are subject to revision: the naming of cis, non-binary, and trans status can highlight and challenge assumed normative status, and I've included cis status when expressed and used by interviewees, some of whom also resisted, questioned, or refused gender pronouns. In her *Legacy* essay, Gill-Peterson reflects on concepts and practices regarding 'deadnaming', which commonly refers to using the name a trans person was given at birth. While acknowledging that this can be a 'useful concept' (Gill-Peterson, J. (2020) 'My Undead Name', *Legacy. A Journal of American Women Writers*. (https://legacywomenwriters.org/2020/09/21/ my-undead-name/ [accessed 22 February 2021]), para 6), Gill-Peterson asks readers to notice how 'it is nevertheless ensnared in this gendered system that obligates each of us to have a clear, consistent, readable gender' (*ibid.*). She observes that the 'demand placed on trans people for consistency and commitment to names and pronouns has the opposite of its intended effect in the outcome. Would-be allies think they are showing that they take trans people's identities seriously by intensely conforming to contemporary conventions, but what they are really saying is *I need you to be legible, clear, and easy for me to understand. I need your gender to make me comfortable.* The system of gendered naming and pronouns itself is completely untouched, untroubled, by this maneuver' (*ibid.*). See also Zaborskis, M. (2022) 'Exploiting Shared Queer Knowledge' in Mahn, C., Brim, B., and Taylor, Y. (eds) *Queer Sharing in the Marketized University*. London: Routledge.

3. Brim, M. (2020) *Poor Queer Studies*. Durham, NC: Duke University Press; Mahn et al. (eds), *Queer Sharing in the Marketized University*; Taylor, Y. and Lahad, K. (eds) (2018) *Feeling Academic in the Neoliberal University: Feminist Flights, Fights and Failures*. Basingstoke: Palgrave; Taylor, Y., Brim, M., and Mahn, C. (2022) *Queer Precarities In and Out of Higher Education*. London: Bloomsbury.

4. These headlines betray recent pasts and ongoing present realities; the Conservative government's allyship of LGBTQ+ groups reads as suspicious in the context of decades of discrimination enshrined in laws like Section 28/Clause 2a (1986/88). The Scottish Government's support of reforms to the Gender Recognition Act 2004 was stalled by a slew of transphobia, including within the Scottish National Party (SNP), and the de-prioritisation of equalities work within the COVID-19 pandemic climate echoes across constituent UK governments. Equality becomes reduced to a diversity showcase, expanded and played out as homonationalist posturing on the global stage, whilst LGBTQ+ groups are chronically underfunded.

5. Davidson, N., Liinpää, M., McBride, M., and Virdee, S. (eds) (2018) *No Problem Here: Understanding Racism in Scotland*. Edinburgh: Luath Press Limited; Ritch, E. (2019) 'Foreboding Newness: Brexit and Feminist Civil Society in Scotland' in Dustin, M., Ferreira, N., and Millns, S. (eds) *Gender and Queer Perspectives on Brexit*, Cham: Palgrave, pp. 333–62.

6. See for example: Connell, R. (2019) *The Good University: What Universities Actually Do and Why It's Time for Radical Change*. London: Zed Books; Taylor, Y. (ed.) (2012) *Educational Diversity: The Subject of Difference and Different Subjects*. Basingstoke: Palgrave; Thwaites, R. and Pressland, A. (eds) (2017) (eds) *Being an Early Career Feminist Academic: Global Perspectives, Experiences, and Challenges*. Basingstoke: Palgrave.

7. Code-switching extends beyond shifting words and often represents a process of racialisation and (not) fitting in, see for example: 'Code-switching: How BAME and LGBT People "Blend In"' (https://www.bbc.co.uk/news/newsbeat-45978770 [accessed 27 October 2018]); Kushins, E.R. (2014) 'Sounding Like Your Race in the Employment Process: An Experiment on Speaker Voice, Race Identification, and Stereotyping', *Race and Social Problems* 6(3): 237–48; Young, V.A. (2014) 'Straight Black Queer: Obama, Code-Switching, and the Gender Anxiety of African American Men', *PMLA* 129(3): 464–70.

8. See for example: Ahmed, S. (2010) *On Being Included: Racism and Diversity in Institutional Life*. Durham, NC: Duke University Press; Bhopal, K. (2018) *White Privilege: The Myth of a Post-Racial Society*. Bristol: Policy Press.

9. D'Emilio, J. (1993) 'Capitalism and Gay Identity' in Abelove, H., Barale, M.A., and Halperin, D.M. (eds), *The Lesbian and Gay Studies Reader*. New York: Routledge, pp. 467–76.

10. Taylor, Y. (2007) *Working-Class Lesbian Life: Classed Outsiders*. Basingstoke: Palgrave.

11. Taylor, Y. (2009) *Lesbian and Gay Parenting: Securing Social and Educational Capital*. Basingstoke: Palgrave.

12. Brim *Poor Queer Studies*.

13. Duggan, L. and Muñoz, J. (2009) 'On Hope and Hopelessness: A Dialogue', *Women and Performance* 19: 2.

14. Rogaly, B. (2020) *Stories from a Migrant City. Living and Working Together in the Shadow of Brexit*. Manchester: Manchester University Press.

15. See for example: Fazio, M., Launius, C., Strangleman, T. (2020) *Routledge International Handbook of Working-Class Studies*. Abingdon: Routledge; Mckenzie, L. (2015) *Getting By: Estates, Class and Culture in Austerity Britain*. Bristol: Policy Press; Tyler, I. (2013) *Revolting Subjects. Social Abjection and Resistance in Neoliberal Britain*. London: Zed.

16. *Queer as Folk* was a 1999 British television series that chronicled the lives of three gay men living in Manchester's gay village around Canal Street, overlapping with 2001 fieldwork.

17. See for example: Eng, L.D. and Puar, K.J. (2020) 'Introduction: Left of Queer', *Social Text* 145: 25–47; Rogaly, B. (2020) *Stories from a Migrant City. Living and Working Together in the Shadow of Brexit*. Manchester: Manchester University Press; Jones, H. (2021) *Violent Ignorance. Confronting Racism and Migration Control*. London: Zed.

18. Puar, J.K. (2007) *Terrorist Assemblages: Homonationalism in Queer Times*. Durham, NC: Duke University Press.

19. Blair, T. (1999) Leader's speech, Bournemouth. *Speech Archive* (http://www.britishpoliticalspeech.org/speech-archive.htm?speech=205 [accessed 16 October 2020]).

20. Taylor, Y. (2005) 'Real Politik or Real Politics? Working-Class Lesbians' Political "Awareness" and Activism', *Women's Studies International Forum* 28(6): 484–94.

21. Taylor, *Lesbian and Gay Parenting*.

22. See for example: Lehtonen, A.C. (2018). '"Helping Workless Families": Cultural Poverty and the Family in Austerity and Anti-welfare Discourse', *Sociological Research Online*, 23(1): 84–99; Tyler, I. (2020) *Stigma. The Machinery of Inequality*. London: Zed.

23. See for example: Duggan, L. (2003) *The Twilight of Equality? Neoliberalism, Cultural Politics, and the Attack on Democracy*. Boston: Beacon Press; Binnie, J. (2004) *The Globalization of Sexuality*. London: SAGE Publications Ltd.

24. See for example: Mukherjee, U. and Barn, R. (2021) 'Concerted Cultivation as a Racial Parenting Strategy: Race, Ethnicity and Middle-class Indian Parents in Britain', *British Journal of Sociology of Education*, 42(4): 521–36; Rollock, N. (2012) '"You Got a Pass, So What More Do You Want?": Race, Class and Gender Intersections in the Educational Experiences of the Black Middle Class', *Race, Ethnicity and Education*, 15: 121–39.

25. Taylor, Y. and Snowdon, R. (eds) (2014) *Queering Religion, Religious Queers*. London: Routledge.

26. See for example: Ammaturo, F.R. (2015) 'The 'Pink Agenda': Questioning and Challenging European Homonationalist Sexual Citizenship', *Sociology*, 49(6): 1151–66; Schulman, S. (2011) 'Israel and "Pinkwashing"', *The New York Times* [accessed 11 November 2020].

27. Berlant, L. (2007) 'On the Case', *Critical Inquiry*, 33(4) (Summer 2007): 663–72, at 666.

28. *Ibid.*, at 670.

CHAPTER 2

1. Puwar, N. (2020) 'Carrying as Method: Listening to Bodies as Archives', *Body & Society*, 27(1): 3–26.

2. UK Research and Innovation (UKRI) funding anticipates that projects will deposit data in the UK Data Archive. The question 'What happens if you do not deposit your data?' is answered with 'You will not be able to submit new funding applications until you have: … deposited your data [and] told UK Data Service where you've published it'. There are risks in (not) depositing data, but particular data is unwanted, exceeding normative codes, categories, and box files. Queer data, by which I mean more than just data about LGBTQ+ people, may become part of this (queer) unwanted (https://www.ukri.org/manage-your-award/publishing-your-research-findings/submit-datasets-if-you-have-funding-from-esrc/ [accessed 18 February 2022]).

3. Taylor, Y., Hines, S. and Casey. M. (eds) (2010) *Theorizing Intersectionality and Sexuality*. London: Palgrave.

4. Puwar, 'Carrying as Method': 5.

5. Puwar, 'Carrying as Method'.

6. I recognise my own location/home/where I'm from as a 'pocket of deprivation': The Scottish Index of Multiple Deprivation (SIMD) confirms this. Drumchapel forms 16 data zones within the SIMD (2016). Fifteen of these 16 data zones are ranked within the 15% most deprived areas in Scotland; eleven of the 16 data zones are within the 5% most deprived zones in Scotland. Life expectancy of males in Drumchapel is

seven years lower than in Glasgow as a whole, and eight years lower for women (Glasgow Centre for Population Health, 2016).

7. The 'Right to Buy' scheme (which gave tenants the right to buy their rented home at a discounted price) was passed in the Housing Act 1980 by the Conservative government. It ended for council and housing association tenants in Scotland on 31 July 2016.

8. See for example: Sobande, S. and hill, l.-r. (2022) *Black Oot Here. Black Lives in Scotland*. London: Bloomsbury; Davidson, N., Liinpää, M., McBride, M., and Virdee, S. (eds) (2018) *No Problem Here. Understanding Racism in Scotland*. Edinburgh: Luath Press Limited.

9. There has been a certain queering of and investment in the term 'weegie' as indicative of liberal politics – this stands against a wider usage of the term, often as an insult: 'Weegie, n. and adj.: A native or inhabitant of Glasgow; a Glaswegian. Bam, n.2: A foolish, annoying, or obnoxious person; (also spec.) a belligerent or disruptive person. Often as a contemptuous form of address' (https://www.scotsman.com/lifestyle/baffie-weegie-18-scottish-words-are-now-dictionary-and-their-meaning-1407401 [accessed 18 September 2019]).

10. See Scottish Census data: https://www.scotlandscensus.gov.uk/census-results/at-a-glance/ethnicity/ [accessed 6 March 2022].

11. For example, see the *Race Equality Framework for Scotland (2016-2030)*. This document aspires to achieve race equality by 2030, across areas such as education and lifelong learning; employability, employment and income; and health and home. It promises a more 'intersectional' approach involving BAME individuals, grassroots organisations, and public sector bodies. The Framework was launched on 21 March 2016 to mark the UN Day for the Elimination of Racial Discrimination. See: https://bemis.org.uk/PDF/race-equality-framework-for-scotland-2016-2030.pdf [accessed 20 January 2020].

In 2021, the Scottish Government published a review of the action plans: https://www.gov.scot/publications/immediate-priorities-plan-race-equality-scotland/documents/ [accessed 3 November 2022].

12. Rogaly, B. (2020) *Stories from a Migrant City. Living and Working Together in the Shadow of Brexit*. Manchester: Manchester University Press.

13. Butler, J. (1993) 'Imitation and Gender Insubordination', in A.H. Abelove, M.A. Barale, and D.M. Halperin (eds), *The Lesbian and Gay Studies Reader*. New York: Routledge, 307–20.

14. See also for example 'Gay-Friendly UK Universities Rated in New 2015 Guide' (https://www.topuniversities.com/student-info/university-news/gay-friendly-uk-universities-rated-new-2015-guide [accessed 5 March 2018]).

15. Skeggs, B. (1997) *Formations of Class and Gender: Becoming Respectable*. London: Sage.

16. For more information on Glasgow Women's Library, see here: https:// womenslibrary.org.uk/. There are other feminist and women's libraries, such as The Women's Library at LSE (the London School of Economics and Political Science), which started out in a converted pub in Westminster (in 1926), as The Library of the London Society for Women's Service (see: https://www.lse.ac.uk/library/collection-highlights/the-womens-library). The Feminist Library, started in 1975, holds a large collection of Women's Liberation Movement literature based in London (see: https://feministlibrary.co.uk/). An international list of libraries dedicated to women and girls is given here: https://blogs.ifla.org/lpa/2019/03/08/libraries-around-the-world-completely-dedicated-to-women/ [accessed 4 November 2022].

17. See the GWL timeline here: https://womenslibrary.org.uk/about-us/our-history/gwl-timeline/#event-_81-parnie-street [accessed 18 February 2022].

18. John, S. and Patrick, A. (1999) *Poverty and Social Exclusion of Lesbians and Gay Men in Glasgow*. Glasgow: Glasgow Women's Library.

19. Brim, M. (2020) *Poor Queer Studies*. Durham, NC: Duke University Press.

20. Etta Dunn is an actor, writer, award-winning publisher, and award-winning poet. The inscription is from the opening lines of 'The Baronets O'Blackness':

> 'An embarrassment o' riches
> thon Scots slave owners hud afore tha abolition.
> A black manservant ance a sign o' wealth, a chattel, a thing tae be
> bocht an sold
> lik a fine bred racehorse ur a sack o' sugar ur baccy
> noo wantin wages. Whit next?'

See: https://www.scotslanguage.com/poetry/5759 [accessed 20 January 2022].

21. 'People Make Glasgow' has been adopted as a city slogan, appearing on a range of websites, souvenirs, and buildings. It's been used by the city council and commercial sites. It has a Facebook, an Instagram, and a Twitter account. See for example: https://peoplemakeglasgow.com/ [accessed 5 March 2020].

CHAPTER 3

1. https://spice-spotlight.scot/2021/06/23/life-in-the-pandemic-for-lesbian-gay-bisexual-transgender-lgbt-people-[in-scotland/ [accessed 18 January 2022].

2. Butler, J. (2004) *Precarious Life: The Powers of Mourning and Violence*. New York: Verso.

3. https://www.gov.uk/government/speeches/pm-address-to-the-nation-on-coronavirus-23-march-2020 [accessed 23 March 2020].

4. See for example: Alexander, C., Weekes-Bernard, D., and Arday, J. (2015) *The school report: Race, education and inequality in contemporary Britain.* London: Runnymede Trust; Bhambra, G. (2017) 'Brexit, Trump, and "Methodological Whiteness": On the Misrecognition of Race and Class', Special Issue: The Trump/Brexit Moment: Causes and Consequences, *British Journal of Sociology*, 68(S1): 214–32.

5. 20% of nursing staff are BAME; 64% of nurses who died were BAME. 44% of medical staff are BAME; 95% of doctors who died were BAME (https://www.bma.org.uk/advice-and-support/covid-19/your-health/covid-19-the-risk-to-bame-doctors).

6. Median annual pay for all full-time employees was £31,285 for the tax year ending 5 April 2021, down 0.6% on the previous year. The dropdown menu allows selection by profession, and the UK average for nurses is listed as £35,971 gross, per annum. The current starting salary for a Band 5 Nurse in the UK is £25,655 per year (minus tax and pensions) (https://www.ons.gov.uk/employmentandlabourmarket/peopleinwork/earningsandworkinghours/bulletins/annualsurvey ofhoursandearnings/2021 [accessed 1 December 2021]).

7. Jones, H. (2021) *Violent Ignorance. Confronting Racism and Migration Control.* London: Zed.

8. See also Dixson, T. and Dixson, R. (2022) 'Little Strokes Fell Great Oaks: Silences, Meaning-Making, and LGBTIQ+ Forced Displacement' in Mahn, C., Brim, M., and Taylor, Y (eds), *Queer Sharing in the Marketized University.* London, New York: Routledge, pp. 153–72.

9. Eddo-Lodge, R. (2017) *Why I'm No Longer Talking to White People about Race.* Bloomsbury.

10. Writers on this include: Ahmed, S. (2017) *Living a Feminist Life.* Durham, NC: Duke University Press; Anzaldúa, G. (1990) 'Bridge, Drawbridge, Sandbar or Island: Lesbians-of-Color Hacienda Alianzas' in Albrech, L. and Brewer, R.M. (eds), *Bridges of Power: Women's Multicultural Alliances.* Philadelphia: New Society, pp. 216–33; Kuntsman, A. and Miyake, E. (2008) *Out of Place. Interrogating Silences in Queerness/Raciality.* York: Raw Nerve Books; Lorde, A. (1984) *Sister Outsider: Essays and Speeches.* New York: The Crossing Press.

11. https://www.huffingtonpost.co.uk/entry/rainbow-flag-nhs-lgbtq-community-co-opting-rainbow-flag_uk_5f47a692c5b6cf66b2b40682 [accessed 21 December 2021].

12. United Nations (2020) *COVID-19 and the Human Rights of LGBTI People.* Retrieved from: https://www.ohchr.org/Documents/Issues/LGBT/LGBT Ipeople.pdf

13. The LGBT Foundation reported that, since COVID-19 restrictions had been in place in the UK, 34% of participants had had medical appointments cancelled, 16% reported not being able to access health care for concerns unrelated to COVID-19, and 23% of participants were concerned about access to medication (LGBT Youth Scotland (2020) *The Impact of LGBT Youth Scotland's Digital Youth Work on Young People.* Retrieved from: https://www.youthlinkscotland.org/media/5686/lgbt-ys-digitalyw-research-report.pdf [accessed 22 September 2021].) Those wanting to access fertility services may experience increases in already lengthy waiting lists. LGBT+ people often do not feel certain or confident in everyday health and social care settings and often have specific concerns about ill health and end-of life decisions. Evidence further suggests that COVID-19 has substantially impacted upon gender affirming treatments and surgery (see: Kidd, J., Jackman, K., Barucco, R., Dworkin, J., Dolezal, C., Navalta, T., ... Bockting, W. (2021) 'Understanding the Impact of the COVID-19 Pandemic on the Mental Health of Transgender and Gender Nonbinary Individuals Engaged in a Longitudinal Cohort Study', *Journal of Homosexuality*, 68(4): 592–611).

14. Young LGBTQI+ groups are more at risk of domestic violence and homelessness. Returning to or being unable to leave an unsafe household impacts younger LGBT+ people more so than other age groups (see: Salerno, J., Williams, N., and Gattamorta, K. (2020) 'LGBTQ Populations: Psychologically Vulnerable Communities in the COVID-19 Pandemic', *Psychological Trauma: Theory, Research, Practice, and Policy*, 12(1): 239–42), with up to one in four LGBTQI+ people experiencing domestic abuse (see: Anderson, S. (2020) 'How COVID-19 is affecting LGBTQIA+ young people living in Scotland'. Retrieved from: https://www.lgbtyouth.org.uk/news/2020/how-covid-19-isaffecting-lgbtqiaplus-young-people-living-in-scotland/ [accessed 22 September 2021]; United Nations, *COVID-19 and the Human Rights of LGBTI People*; Viney, D. (2020) *Impact of COVID-19 on LGBT Communities*. Birmingham LGBT. Retrieved from: https://blgbt.org/wp-content/uploads/2020/09/Impact-of-Covid-19-on-LGBTcommunity.pdf [accessed 22 September 2021])). The LGBT Foundation found that out of a total of 555 responses, 9% of BAME LGBT people, 15% of disabled LGBT people, and 17% of both trans and non-binary people did not feel safe where they were staying at the time the survey was carried out (LGBT Youth Scotland, *The Impact of LGBT Youth Scotland's Digital Youth Work on Young People*).

15. See for example: Bradway, T. and Freeman, E. (2022) *Queer Kinship: Race, Sex, Belonging*. Durham: Duke University Press; Weeks, J. (2007) *The World We Have Won. The Remaking of Erotic and Intimate Life*. London: Routledge; Weston, K. (1991) *Families We Choose: Lesbians, Gays, Kinship*. New York: Columbia University Press; Taylor, Y. (2009) *Lesbian*

and Gay Parenting: Securing Social and Educational Capital. Basingstoke: Palgrave.

16. In July 2018, the UK Government published a consultation on reform of the Gender Recognition Act 2004 in England and Wales, also supported by the First Minister of Scotland, Nicola Sturgeon. Reform would make it easier for people to legally change their gender. Action has been repeatedly delayed due to the coronavirus pandemic, as well as significant opposition to the changes, including by 'gender critical' lobby For Women Scotland. On 28 October 2020, the House of Commons Women and Equalities Committee launched an inquiry, and following this, the UK Government declared that it does not intend to change the criteria or recognise non-binary gender.

17. See: Ghaziani, A. (2008) *The Dividends of Dissent: How Conflict and Culture Work in Lesbian and Gay Marches on Washington.* Chicago: University of Chicago Press; Stillwagon, R. and Ghaziani, A. (2019) 'Queer Pop-Ups: A Cultural Innovation in Urban Life', *City & Community*, 18(3): 874–95; Miles, S. (2021) 'After/Lives: Insights from the COVID-19 Pandemic for Gay Neighborhoods' in Bitterman, A. and Hess, D.B. (eds), *The Life and Afterlife of Gay Neighborhoods: Renaissance and Resurgence.* The Urban Book Series. Cham: Springer.

18. Miles, 'After/Lives'.

19. See Big Door Brigade: https://bigdoorbrigade.com/what-is-mutual-aid/ [accessed 8 December 2021].

20. Arani, A. (2020) 'Mutual Aid and Its Ambivalences: Lessons from Sick and Disabled Trans and Queer People of Color', *Feminist Studies*, 46(3): 653–62.

21. Mutual Aid Trans Edinburgh (MATE) compiled a list of useful Mutual Aid information and resources here: https://matedinburgh.wordpress.com/resources/ [accessed 21 February 2021]. Alexia Arani (2020) provides another list here: 'It's Going Down', https://itsgoingdown.org/c19-mutual-aid [accessed 8 December 2021).

22. Supported at least in part through crowdfunding, Kafe Kweer hosts events such as an exhibition series and clothes swaps, as well as hosting a monthly Kweer Kraft Market, including entertainment programmes with tarot card readings, drag, cabaret, variety shows, and so on. Pink Peacock describes itself as a queer, Yiddish, pay-what-you-can cafe in Glasgow's Southside, 'with everyone welcome (except cops and terfs)'. Pink Peacock's anarchist stance and 'Fuck the Police' merchandise attracted mixed feelings within the surrounding community, with an increased police presence unwelcomed in the mixed working-class area, home to higher than city average numbers of minority ethnic populations (see: https://pinkpeacock.gay/). Pink Peacock has itself been subject to

violence, suspected hate crimes, including antisemitism, and wider community experiences of displacement.

23. See Brodie, L. and Heatherington, L. (2022) 'Permeable Spaces: Creating Structured Yet Fluid Cultural Experiences for LGBTI+ Elders' in Taylor, Y., Brim, M., and Mahn, C. (eds), *Queer Precarities in and out of Higher Education*. Bloomsbury.

24. Kuntsman, A. and Miyake, E. (2008) *Out of Place. Interrogating Silences in Queerness/Raciality*. York: Raw Nerve Books.

CHAPTER 4

1. Eng, L.D. and Puar, K.J. (2020) 'Introduction: Left of Queer', *Social Text*, 145: 25–47.

2. Downing, L. and Gillet, R. (eds) (2011) *Queer in Europe. Contemporary Case Studies*. London: New York.

3. See for example: Boyd, C. and Morrison, J. (2014) *Scottish Independence: A Feminist Response*. Edinburgh: Word Power Books; Davidson, N., Liinpää, M., McBride, M., and Virdee, S. (eds) (2018) *No Problem Here: Understanding Racism in Scotland*. Edinburgh: Luath Press Limited.

4. See for example: Erel, U. (2010) 'Migrating Cultural Capital: Bourdieu in Migration Studies', *Sociology*, 44(4): 642–60; Rogaly, B. (2020) *Stories from a Migrant City: Living and Working Together in the Shadow of Brexit*. Manchester: Manchester University Press.

5. Bhambra, G. (2017) 'Brexit, Trump, and "Methodological Whiteness": on the Misrecognition of Race and Class', Special Issue: The Trump/Brexit Moment: Causes and Consequences, *British Journal of Sociology*, 68:S1, 214–32.

6. The accounts in this chapter come from the EU-ESRC Norface consortium-funded project *Comparing Intersectional Lifecourse Inequalities Amongst LGBTQI+ Citizens in Four European Countries* (CILIA) (2018–21). Colleagues working on this grant included: Yener Bayramoglu, María do Mar Castro Varela (Berlin); Sait Bayrakdar, Andrew King (England); Rita Alcaire, Ana Cristina Santos, Ana Lucia Santos (Portugal); myself, Maja B. Andreasen, Claire Goodfellow, Matson Lawrence (Scotland). Over the course of this project the number of EU partner countries (England, Germany, Portugal and Scotland) decreased by two as Scotland and England left the EU. The project was imagined in part to surpass the 'methodological nationalism' of using national frames, references, and places to locate and include populations. Methodological nationalism means the Global North becomes both the starting- and the end-point – a heroic measure of progression now arrived at and via LGBTQ+ rights. These stories, which travel and take up space, disappear the histories of

production into the present, including in the constitution and creation of knowledge. International projects continue to be monitored through and accountable to national institutions: some international partners may have more or less financial backing than others, and may also be implicated in both the reproduction and transformation of living and working conditions and intersectional inequalities. Similarly, country context might be variously depicted as 'diverse' or 'homogenous', as central or peripheral, and as (not) having a place or contribution in the context of research and researchers going 'everywhere'. The research partnerships in the grant were – and are – a long time in the making. So too are the very conditions and categories – intersectional inequalities in the context of LGBTQI+ citizenship across and within borders – that the project worked through.

7. Dorling, D. (2016) 'Brexit: The Decision of a Divided Country', Danny Dorling's Website. Available at: http://www.dannydorling.org/?p=5568 [accessed 21 December 2021].

8. Ahmed, S. (2010) *On Being Included: Racism and Diversity in Institutional Life*. Durham, NC: Duke University Press.

9. Guyan, K. (2022) *Queer Data. Using Gender, Sex and Sexuality Data for Action*. London: Bloomsbury.

   See for example: Bowleg, L. (2008) 'When Black + Lesbian + Woman = Black Lesbian Woman: The Methodological Challenges of Qualitative and Quantitative Intersectionality Research', *Sex Roles*, 59: 312–25; Hunter, M.A. (2010) 'All the Gays are White and all the Blacks are Straight: Black Gay Men, Identity and Community', *Sex Research & Social Policy*, 7: 81–92; Mahn, C. (2019) 'Black Scottish Writing and the Fiction of Diversity' in Breeze, M., Taylor, Y., and Costa, C. (eds), *Time and Space in the Neoliberal University*. Basingstoke: Palgrave.

10. See for example: Anzaldúa, G. (1991) 'To(o) Queer the Writer-Loca, escritora y chicana' in Warland, B. (ed.), *Inversions: Writing by Dykes, Queers, and Lesbians*. Vancouver: Press Gang Publishers, pp. 249–63; Kuntsman, A. and Miyake, E. (2008) *Out of Place. Interrogating Silences in Queerness/Raciality*. York: Raw Nerve Books; LeBel, S. (2021) 'Lesbian Processing at the End of the World: Lesbian Identity and Queer Environmental Futurity', *Journal of Lesbian Studies*, 26(2):159–73.

11. The 2011 Census data used a standardised list of 18 ethnic groups: https://www.ethnicity-facts-figures.service.gov.uk/style-guide/ethnic-groups#list-of-ethnic-groups

12. https://www.ons.gov.uk/peoplepopulationandcommunity/cultural identity/sexuality/bulletins/sexualidentityuk/2019#:~:text= An%20estimated%201.4%20million%20people%20aged%2016%20years %20and%20over,as%20bisexual%20(Figure%201) [accessed 1 March 2020]. In estimations of the UK trans population, the Government

Equalities Office document 'Trans in the UK' simply states, 'We don't know. No robust data on the UK trans population exists. We tentatively estimate that there are approximately 200,000–500,000 trans people in the UK. The Office for National Statistics is researching whether and how to develop a population estimate' (https://assets.publishing.service.gov.uk/government/uploads/system/uploads/attachment_data/file/721642/GEO-LGBT-factsheet.pdf [accessed 25 February 2022]).

13. Sibley, C.G., Houkamau, C.A., and Hoverd, W.J. (2011) 'Ethnic Group Labels and Intergroup Attitudes in New Zealand: Naming Preferences Predict Distinct Ingroup and Outgroup Biases', *Analyses of Social Issues and Public Policy*, 11(1): 201–20.

14. Zabrowskis, M. (2022) 'Exploiting shared queer knowledge' in Mahn, C., Brim, M., and Taylor, Y (eds), *Queer Sharing in the Marketized University*. London: Routledge.

15. Mackay, F. (2021) *Female Masculinities and the Gender Wars. The Politics of Sex*. London: Bloomsbury.

16. Skeggs, B. (1997) *Formations of Class and Gender: Becoming Respectable*. London: Sage; Fazio, M., Launius, C., and Strangleman, T. (2020) *Routledge International Handbook of Working-Class Studies*. Abingdon: Routledge.

17. Puar, J.K. (2013) 'Rethinking Homonationalism', *International Journal of Middle East Studies*, 45: 336–39.

18. Petzen, J. (2012) 'Contesting Europe: A Call for an Anti-Modern Sexual Politics', *European Journal of Women's Studies*, 19(1): 97–114. See also Ayoub, P. and Paternotte, D. (2014) *LGBT Activism and the Making of Europe. A Rainbow Europe?* London: Palgrave.

19. Traies, J. (ed.) (2021) 'Free To Be Me', *Refugee Stories from the Lesbian Immigration Support Group*. UK: Tollington Press.

20. See for example: Davidson et al (eds), *No Problem Here*; Mahn, C. 'Black Scottish Writing and the Fiction of Diversity'; Sobande, F. and hill, l. (2022) *Black oot here: black lives in Scotland. Blackness in Britain*. London: Bloomsbury.

21. See for example: Binnie, J. (2004) *The Globalization of Sexuality*. London: SAGE Publications Ltd; Haritaworn, J. (2015) *Queer Lovers and Hateful Others: Regenerating Violent Times and Places*. London: Pluto.

22. Arondekar, A. and Patel, G. (2016) 'Area Impossible: Notes Toward an Introduction', *GLQ: A Journal of Lesbian and Gay Studies*, 22(2): 151–71; Eng & Puar, 'Introduction: Left of Queer'.

23. Anzaldúa, G. (1990) 'Bridge, Drawbridge, Sandbar or Island: Lesbians-of-Color Hacienda Alianzas', in Albrech, L. and Brewer, R.M. (eds), *Bridges of Power: Women's Multicultural Alliances*. Philadelphia: New Society, pp. 216–33; Rajan-Rankin, S. (2017) 'Brexit Logics: Myths and Fact – A Black Feminist Analysis', *feminists@law*. University of Kent. Available

at: http://journals.kent.ac.uk/index.php/feministsatlaw/article/view/423 [accessed 6 May 2022].

24. Scotland – and the Scottish National Party in particular – has seen a resurgence in transphobic rhetoric, made mainstream in politicians' public comments in the wake of the 2019 public consultation on the Gender Recognition Act (GRA) 2004. (See, for example, 'SNP Transphobia Row: Why has Nicola Sturgeon's Party been Accused of "Transphobic Views"?': https://www.scotsman.com/news/people/snp-transphobia-row-why-has-nicola-sturgeons-party-been-accused-transphobic-views-and-who-teddy-hope-3117850 [accessed 1 April 2022].)

25. Lawrence, M. and Taylor, Y. (2019) 'The UK Government LGBT Action Plan: Discourses of Progress, Enduring Stasis, and LGBTQI+ Lives "Getting Better"', *Critical Social Policy*, 40(4): 586–607.

26. Boyd, C. and Morrison, J. (2014) *Scottish Independence. A Feminist Response*. Edinburgh: Word Power Books.

27. Patel, T. and Connelly, L. (2019) '"Post-race" Racisms in the narratives of "Brexit" Voters', *The Sociological Review*, 67(5): 968–84.

CHAPTER 5

1. See for example: Forket, K. (2017) *Austerity as a Public Mood: Social Anxieties and Social Struggles*. Rowman & Littlefield Publisher; Lehtonen, A.C. (2018) 'Helping Workless Families: Cultural Poverty and the Family in Austerity and Anti-Welfare Discourse' *Sociological Research Online*, 23(1), 84–99; Tyler, I. (2013) *Revolting Subjects. Social Abjection and Resistance in Neoliberal Britain*. London: Zed; Tyler, I. (2020) *Stigma. The Machinery of Inequality*. London: Zed.

2. Butler, J. (2004) *Precarious Life: The Powers of Mourning and Violence*. New York: Verso; Gleeson, J.J. and O'Rooke, E. (eds) (2021) *Transgender Marxism*. London: Pluto; Raha, N. (2021) 'A Queer Marxist Transfeminism: Queer and Trans Social Reproduction' in *Marxism ibid.*, pp. 85–115.

3. See for example in: Mahn, C., Brim, M., and Taylor, Y. (eds) *Queer Sharing in the Marketized University*. Palgrave; Taylor, Y., Brim, M., and Mahn, C. (eds) *Queer Precarities in and out of Higher Education*. London: Bloomsbury.

4. Bhattacharyya, G. (2015) *Crisis, Austerity and Everyday Life, Living in a Time of Diminishing Expectations*. London: Palgrave.

5. Hakim, J. Chatzidakis, A., Littler, J., and Rottenberg, C. (2020) *The Care Manifesto: The Politics of Interdependence*. London: Verso; Spade,

D. (2020) *Mutual Aid: Building Solidarity During the Crisis*. New York: Verso.

6. See for example: Taylor, Y. (ed.) (2012) *Educational Diversity: The Subject of Difference and Different Subjects*. Basingstoke: Palgrave; Taylor, Y. (ed.) (2014) *The Entrepreneurial University. Public Engagements, Intersecting Impacts*. Basingstoke: Palgrave; Breeze, M. and Taylor, Y. (2020) *Feminist Repetitions in Higher Education*. Cham, Switzerland: Palgrave; Addison, M., Breeze, B., and Taylor, Y. (2022) *The Palgrave Handbook of Imposter Syndrome in Higher Education*. Cham, Switzerland: Palgrave.

7. See for example: Taylor, Y. and Lahad, K. (eds) (2018) *Feeling Academic in the Neoliberal University: Feminist Flights, Fights and Failures*, Basingstoke: Palgrave; Connell, R. (2019) *The Good University: What Universities Actually Do and Why It's Time for Radical Change*. London: Zed Books.

8. Savage, M. (2016) 'The Fall and Rise of Class Analysis in British Sociology', 1950–2016', *Tempo Social*, 28(2): 57–72.

9. Nash, J. (2019) *Black Feminism Reimagined. After Intersectionality*. Durham, NC: Duke University Press.

10. Autostraddle, 'UK LGBT Politics Crash Course: What Austerity and the Far Right Mean For Queers' (https://www.autostraddle.com/uk-lgbt-politics-crash-course-what-austerity-and-the-far-right-mean-for-queers-219163/ [accessed 1 February 2018]).

11. Pitt (Cohen), J. and Monk, S. (2016) '"We build a wall around our sanctuaries": Queerness and Precarity', Novara Media https://novaramedia.com/2016/08/28/we-build-a-wall-around-our-sanctuaries-queerness-as-precarity/ [accessed 3 January 2016]).

12. See for example: Binnie, J. (2004) *The Globalization of Sexuality*. SAGE Publications Ltd; Pellegrini, A. (2002) 'Consuming Lifestyle: Commodity Capitalism and Transformations in Gay Identity' in Cruz-Malame, A. and Maralansen IV, M.F. (eds) *Queer Globalisations: Citizenship and the Afterlife of Colonialism*. New York: NYU Press, pp. 134–45; Taylor, Y. and Falconer, E. (2015) '"Seedy Bars and Grotty Pints": Close Encounters in Queer Leisure Spaces', *Social and Cultural Geography*, 16(1), 43–57.

13. Peñaloza, L. (2008) 'We're Here, We're Queer, and We're Going Shopping' in Jacobsen. J. and Zeller, A. (eds), *Queer Economics*. London: Routledge, pp. 304–29.

14. Tyler, I. (2013) *Revolting Subjects. Social Abjection and Resistance in Neoliberal Britain*. London: Zed; see also Brewis, J. and Jack, G. (2010) 'Consuming Chavs: The Ambiguous Politics of Gay Chavinism', *Sociology*, 44(2): 251–68.

15. There is variation in the legislation for different parts of the UK: the Marriage (Same Sex Couples) Act 2013, in England and Wales, and the Marriage and Civil Partnership (Scotland) Act 2014 both came into force in March 2014. Northern Ireland legislated for same-sex marriage

through the Northern Ireland (Executive Formation etc) Act 2019, coming into force in January 2020.

16. Skeggs, B. (1997) *Formations of Class and Gender: Becoming Respectable*. London: Sage; Mckenzie, L. (2015) *Getting By: Estates, Class and Culture in Austerity Britain*. Bristol: Policy Press.

17. Cohen, C.J. (1997) 'Punks, Bulldaggers and Welfare Queens: The Radical Potential of Queer Politics', *GLQ*, 3: 437–65.

18. Weston, K. (1991) *Families We Choose: Lesbians, Gays, Kinship*. New York: Columbia University Press; Weeks., J., Heaphy, B., and Donovan, C. (2001) *Same Sex Intimacies. Families of Choice and Other Life Experiments*. London: Routledge.

19. The ban on conversion therapy represents a recent example of religion and sexuality being positioned as oppositional forces, despite religious leaders, inter-faith groups, and, for example, Muslim MP Afzal Khan also noting support for the ban. See also: 'Christian leaders overwhelmingly support full ban on "conversion therapy"', *Open Table Network* (https://opentable.lgbt/our-news/2022/2/28/christian-leaders-overwhelmingly-support-full-ban-on-conversion-therapy [accessed 22 February 2022]). The UK Government committed to end the practice of conversion therapy in the UK via their LGBT Action Plan (2018); in 2022 the UK Government decided not to include trans people in a proposed ban on conversion practices in England and Wales, while the Scottish Government has said the ban will include sexuality and gender identity. Conversion therapy has medical and secular legacies that are somewhat effaced in locating this practice solely in (often certain) religions (see Taylor, Y. and Snowdon, R. (eds) (2014) *Queering Religion, Religious Queers*. London: Routledge).

20. Cuthbert, K. and Taylor, Y. (2018) 'Queer Liveability: Inclusive Church-Scenes', *Sexualities*, 22(5-6): 951–68.

21. See for example: Taylor and Snowdon (eds) *Queering Religion, Religious Queers*; Taylor, Y. (2015) *Making Space for Queer Identifying Youth*. Basingstoke: Palgrave; Page, S. and Shipley, H. (2020) *Religion and Sexualities. Theories, Themes and Methodologies*. Routledge: New York; Wilcox, M. (2003) *Coming Out in Christianity: Religion, Identity, and Community*. Indiana: Indiana University Press.

22. The original Metropolitan Community Church was founded in Los Angeles in 1968 by Troy Perry, a former Pentecostal pastor who had been defrocked in the early 1960s for being gay. Perry's founding of MCC was intended to open up a gay-affirming and inclusive space of worship for same-sex-attracted Christians. See: http://mcchurch.org/files/2009/08/MCC-GLOBAL-PRESENCE-as-of-June-23-2012.pdf [accessed 9 September 2017].

23. See also: Counts, S. (2022) 'Queer Kinship and the Practice of Faith During COVID-19' in Taylor et al (eds) *Queer Precarities in and out of Higher Education*.
24. Page & Shipley, *Religion and Sexualities. Theories, Themes and Methodologies*.
25. While Estelle speaks pragmatically about school choices, religious schools have often been identified as sites of trouble for LGBTQ+ youth. The UK government's recent allocation of funding to the charities Stonewall and Barnardo's to tackle homophobia, biphobia, and transphobia in faith schools demonstrates the linking of these sites as particularly problematic. This occurs amidst concerns over 'British values' and the increasing mobilisation of 'sexual orientation equality' rhetoric as part of these racist, nationalist, and often specifically anti-Islam discourses: Cuthbert and Taylor, 'Queer Liveability: Inclusive Church-Scenes'.
26. Berlant, L. (2011) *Cruel Optimism*. Durham, NC: Duke University Press; Eng, L.D. and Puar, K.J. (2020) 'Introduction: Left of Queer', *Social Text*, 145: 25–47; Mahn et al *Queer Sharing in the Marketized University*; Taylor et al (eds), *Queer Precarities in and out of Higher Education*.

CHAPTER 6

1. Ahmed, S. (2017) *Living a Feminist Life*. Durham, NC: Duke University Press.
2. Liu, P. (2020) 'Queer Theory and the Spectre of Materialism', *Social Text*, 145: 24–57.
3. Halberstam, J. (2011) *The Queer Art of Failure*. Durham, NC: Duke University Press.
4. Haritaworn, J. (2008) 'Shifting Positionalities: Empirical Reflections on a Queer/Trans of Colour Methodology', *Sociological Research Online*, 13(1): n.p., http://www.socresonline.org.uk/13/1/13.html [accessed 3 May 2022]).
5. Dunne, G. (1997) *Lesbian Lifestyles: Women's Work and the Politics of Sexuality*. Basingstoke: Palgrave; Weeks., J., Heaphy, B., and Donovan, C. (2001) *Same Sex Intimacies*. London: Routledge.
6. Ahmed, *Living a Feminist Life*.
7. See for example: Escudero-Alías, M. (2021) 'The Institutionalization of Queer Theory: Where has Lesbian Criticism Gone?', *Journal of Lesbian Studies*, DOI: 10.1080/10894160.2021.2003515 [accessed 28 April 2022]; Freeman, E. (2021) 'Committed to the End: On Caretaking, Rereading, and Queer Theory' in Herring, S. and Wallace, L. (eds), *Long Term. Essays on Commitment*. Durham, NC: Duke University Press, pp. 24–55.
8. See for example: Anzaldúa, G. (1990) 'Bridge, Drawbridge, Sandbar or Island: Lesbians-of-Color Hacienda Alianzas' in Albrech, L. and

Brewer, R.M. (eds), *Bridges of Power: Women's Multicultural Alliances.* Philadelphia: New Society, pp. 216–33; hooks, b. (1994) *Teaching to Transgress: Education as the Practice of Freedom.* New York: Routledge; hooks, b. (2000) *Feminism in for Everybody.* London: Pluto; hooks, b. (2000) *Where We Stand: Class Matters.* New York: Routledge; Moraga, C. and Anzaldúa, G. (1984) *This Bridge Called My Back: Radical Writings by Women of Color.* Kitchen Table Women of Color Press.

9. 'The Combahee River Collective Statement', reproduced in Sharpley-Whiting, J. (ed.) (2000) *The Black Feminist Reader.* Oxford: Blackwell Publishers Ltd, pp. 261–270. (Also available at: https://careprogram.ucla.edu/education/readings/Combahee/1977).

10. *Ibid.*, p. 281.

11. Anzaldúa, G. (1991) 'To(o) Queer the Writer-Loca, escritora y chicana' in Warland, B. (ed), *Inversions: Writing by Dykes, Queers, and Lesbians.* Vancouver: Press Gang Publishers, pp. 242–63.

12. See for example: Cauthern, C.R. (1979) '900 Black Lesbians Speak', *Off Our Backs*, 9(6): 12; Frankenberg, R. (1993) *White Women, Race Matters. The Social Construction of Whiteness.* Minneapolis: University of Minnesota Press; Nash, J. (2019) *Black Feminism Reimagined. After Intersectionality.* Durham, NC: Duke University Press.

13. Kuntsman, A. and Miyake, E. (2008) *Out of Place. Interrogating Silences in Queerness/Raciality.* York: Raw Nerve Books.

14. Bhambra, G. (2007) *Rethinking Modernity: Postcolonialism and the Sociological Imagination.* Oxford: Berg; Bowleg, L. (2008) 'When Black + Lesbian + Woman = Black Lesbian Woman: The Methodological Challenges of Qualitative and Quantitative Intersectionality Research', *Sex Roles*, 59: 312–25.

15. *Rebel Dykes* is described as: 'A brilliant and refreshing story of UK post-punk dyke culture, told by those who lived it, in all their ass-kicking, leather-wearing glory. The film follows a tight-knit group of friends who met at Greenham Common peace camp and went on to become artists, performers, musicians and activists in London. A heady mash-up of animation, archive footage and interviews tells the story of a radical scene: squatters, BDSM nightclubs, anti-Thatcher rallies, protests demanding action around AIDS and the fierce ties of chosen family. This is an extraordinarily privileged glimpse into a bygone world by those who not only lived out their politics with heartfelt conviction but lived to tell the tale' (https://www.bfi.org.uk/flare/films/rebel-dykes [accessed 7 February 2022]). Elizabeth Freeman summarises the challenges and possibilities of re-creating LGBT presence as involving 'eclectic, idiosyncratic, and transient archives including performances, gossip, found objects and methods (or anti-methods) that rely on counter-intuitive juxtapositions

of events or materials' (Freeman, E. (2007) 'Introduction', *GLQ: A Journal of Lesbian and Gay Studies*, 13(2–3): 159–76: 162).

16. Butler, J. (1990) *Gender Trouble: Feminism and the Subversion of Identity.* New York: Routledge.

17. Keating, S. (2017) 'Can lesbian identity survive the gender revolution?' Buzzfeed News. (https://www.buzzfeednews.com/article/shannonkeating/can-lesbian-identity-survive-the-gender-revolution [accessed 27 April 2022]).

18. Vincent, B., Erikainen, S., and Pearce, R. (2020) *TERF Wars: Feminism and the Fight for Transgender Futures.* London: Sage.

19. Duggan, L. and Hunter, N. (1995) *Sex Wars: Sexual Dissent and Political Culture.* New York: Routledge; Nash, J. (2019) *Black Feminism Reimagined. After Intersectionality.* Durham, NC: Duke University Press.

20. The Lesbian, Gay and Bisexual Alliance emerged from the Gender Recognition Act 2019 consultation with desires to #presspause on and halt reform. In dropping the 'T' from the widely used LGBT+ acronym, this group demarcated political boundaries, with others responding in turn, via hashtags such as #LwiththeT, #GwiththeT, #BwiththeT, demonstrating trans-inclusion and allyship.

21. Gill-Peterson, J. (2022) 'Toward a Historiography of the Lesbian Transsexual, or the TERF's Nightmare', *Journal of Lesbian Studies*, DOI: 10.1080/10894160.2021.1979726.

22. Escudero-Alías, M. (2021) 'The Institutionalization of Queer Theory: Where has Lesbian Criticism Gone?', *Journal of Lesbian Studies*, DOI: 10.1080/10894160.2021.2003515 [accessed 28 April 2022].

23. Crisp, C. (2014) 'White and Lesbian: Intersections of Privilege and Oppression', *Journal of Lesbian Studies*, 18(2): 106–117.

24. Dottolo, A.L. (2014) 'Introduction: Special Issue on Lesbians and White Privilege', *Journal of Lesbian Studies*, 18(2): 101–105.

25. Crisp, 'White and Lesbian'.

26. Gleeson, J.J. and O'Rooke, E. (2021) *Transgender Marxism.* London: Pluto.

27. Puwar, N. (2004) *Space Invaders: Race, Gender and Bodies Out of Place.* London: Bloomsbury. See also: Jones, H. (2021) *Violent Ignorance: Confronting Racism and Migration Control.* London: Zed.

28. Siraj, A. (2018) 'British Pakistani Lesbians Existing Within the Confines of the Closet', *Culture, Health & Sexuality*, 20(1): 23–89.

29. Falconer, E. and Taylor, Y. (2017) 'Negotiating Queer and Religious Identities in Higher Education: Queering 'Progression' in the 'University Experience', *British Journal of Sociology of Education*, 38(6): 782–97.

30. See for example: Davidson, N., Liinpää, M., McBride, M., and Virdee, S. (eds) (2018) *No Problem Here. Understanding Racism in Scotland.* Edinburgh: Luath Press Limited; Sobande, F. and hill, l. (2022) 'Black

Oot Here: Black Lives in Scotland' in *Blackness in Britain*. London: Bloomsbury.

31. Nayak, A. (2003) *Race, Place and Globalization: Youth Cultures in a Changing World*. Oxford: Berg.

32. See for example: Ahmed, S. (1997) '"It's a sun tan, isn't it?": Auto-Biography as an Identificatory Practice' in Mirza, H. (ed.) *Black British Feminism: A Reader*. London and New York: Routledge, pp. 153–167; Caballero, C. and Aspinall, P. (2018) *Mixed Race Britain in the Twentieth Century*. London: Palgrave; Mahn, C. (2019) 'Black Scottish Writing and the Fiction of Diversity' in Breeze, M., Taylor, Y. and Costa, C. (eds), *Time and Space in the Neoliberal University*. Basingstoke: Palgrave.

33. Eng, L.D. and Puar, K.J. (2020) 'Introduction: Left of Queer', *Social Text*, 145: 24–57.

CHAPTER 7

1. Raffo, S. (1997) *Queerly Classed*. Boston: South End Press.

2. Brim, M. (2020) *Poor Queer Studies*. Durham, NC: Duke University Press; Taylor, Y. (2007) *Working-Class Lesbian Life: Classed Outsiders*. Basingstoke: Palgrave; Taylor, Y. (2009) *Lesbian and Gay Parenting: Securing Social and Educational Capital*. Basingstoke: Palgrave.

3. Federici, S. (2017) 'Capitalism and the Struggle against Sexual Work' in Federici, S. and Austin, A. *The New York Wages for Housework Committee, 1972–1976: History, Theory and Documents*. New York: Autonomedia, pp. 144–6; Federici, S. (2019) *Re-Enchanting the World: Feminism and the Politics of the Commons*. Toronto: PM.

4. On the blog post '"We've been organising like this since day" – why we must remember the Black roots of mutual aid groups', Eshe Kiama Zuri writes, '[a]s the black founder of a radical mutual aid group launched in 2018, I am frustrated to see new, white, middle-class mutual aid groups launched during the pandemic bulldozing pre-existing networks': https://gal-dem.com/weve-been-organising-like-this-since-day-why-we-must-remember-the-black-roots-of-mutual-aid-groups/ [accessed 1 March 2022].

5. The texts referred to in this example reading list are set out in the Appendix to this book.

6. Anzaldúa, G. (1991) 'To(o) Queer the Writer-Loca, Escritora y Chicana' in Warland, B. (ed.) *Inversions: Writing by Dykes, Queers, and Lesbians*. Vancouver: Press Gang Publishers, pp. 249–63.

7. Ahmed, S. (2017) *Living a Feminist Life*. Durham, NC: Duke University Press; Gunaratnam, Y. (2021) 'Presentation Fever and Podium Effects', *Feminist Theory*, 22(4): 497–517; Puwar, N. (2020) 'Carrying as Method: Listening to Bodies as Archives', *Body & Society* 27(1): 3–26.

8. Addison, M., Breeze, B., and Taylor, Y. (2022) *The Palgrave Handbook of Imposter Syndrome in Higher Education*. Cham, Switzerland: Palgrave.
9. Lorber, J. (1997) *The Variety of Feminisms and their Contribution to Gender Equality*. Oldenburg: BIS, Bibliotheks- und Informationssystem der Universität Oldenburg (https://diglib.bis.uni-oldenburg.de/pub/unireden/ur97/kap1.pdf [accessed 4 March 2022]).
10. Breeze, M. and Taylor, Y. (2020) *Feminist Repetitions in Higher Education*. Cham, Switzerland: Palgrave.
11. Eng, L.D. and Puar, K.J. (2020) 'Introduction: Left of Queer', *Social Text*, 145: 1–25; Gleeson, J.J. and O'Rooke, E. (2021) *Transgender Marxism*. London: Pluto; Liu, P. (2020) 'Queer Theory and the Spectre of Materialism', *Social Text*, 145: 25–47; Raffo, *Queerly Classed*.
12. Eng & Puar 'Introduction: Left of Queer'.
13. Freeman, E. (2021) 'Committed to the End: On Caretaking, Rereading, and Queer Theory' in Herring, S. and Wallace, L. (eds) *Long Term. Essays on Commitment*. Durham, NC: Duke University Press, pp. 25–45, at 33.
14. Ahmed, *Living a Feminist Life*.
15. Hemmings, C. (2011) *Why Stories Matter. The Political Grammar of Feminist Theory*. Durham, NC: Duke University Press; Olufemi, L. (2020) *Feminism Interrupted. Disrupting Power*. London: Pluto.
16. Love, H. (2015) 'Doing Being Deviant: Deviance Studies, Description, and the Queer Ordinary', *Differences. A Journal of Feminist Cultural Studies*, 26(1):74–95; Love, H. (2021) *Underdogs. Social Deviance and Queer Theory*. Chicago: Chicago University Press.
17. See for example: Kuhar, R. and Paternotte, D. (2017) *Anti-Gender Campaigns in Europe: Mobilizing Against Equality*. London: Rowan & Littlefield; Paternotte, D. (2019) 'Gender Studies and the Dismantling of Critical Knowledge in Europe: Assaults on Gender Studies are Part of an Attack on Democracy' (https://www.aaup.org/article/gender-studies-and-dismantling-critical-knowledge-europe#.YiHhyRDP3Xo [accessed 4 March 2022]).
18. See for example: Jackson, S. (1999) *Heterosexuality in Question*. London: Sage; Plummer, K. (1975) *Sexual Stigma: An Interactionist Account*. London: Routledge; Weeks, J. (2007) *The World We Have Won. The Remaking of Erotic and Intimate Life*. London: Routledge.
19. Dorothy Allison's work includes for example: Allison, D. (1988) *Trash: Short Stories*. Firebrand Books; Allison., D. (1992) *Bastard Out of Carolina*. New York: Penguin; Allison, D. (1994) *Skin: Talking About Sex, Class & Literature*. New York: Firebrand Books; Allison, D. (1995) *Two or Three Things I Know for Sure*. New York: Penguin.
20. Tea, M. (1998) *The Passionate Mistakes and Intricate Corruption of One Girl in America*. New York: Autonomedi; Tea, M. (2017) 'Pigeon Manifesto' in Olson, A. (ed.) *Work Warriors*. Emeryville, CA: Seal Press;

Tea, M. (ed) (2004) *Without a Net: The Female Experience of Growing Up Working Class.* Emeryville, CA: Seal Press; Bechdel, A. (1983–2008) *Dykes to Watch Out For* (https://dykestowatchoutfor.com/dtwof/ [accessed 28 April 2022]); Bechdel, A. (2021) *The Secret to Superhuman Strength.* Vintage Publishing; DiMassa, D. (1993) *The Complete Hothead Paisan: Homicidal Lesbian Terrorist.* Cleis Press.

21. Bannon, A. (1957) *Odd Girl Out.* New York: Gold Medal Books.
22. Skeggs, B. (1997) *Formations of Class and Gender: Becoming Respectable.* London: Sage.
23. hooks, b. (1994) *Teaching to Transgress: Education as the Practice of Freedom.* New York: Routledge; hooks, b. (2000) *Feminism is for Everybody.* London: Pluto; hooks, b. (2000) *Where We Stand: Class Matters.* New York: Routledge; hooks, b. (2003) *Teaching Community: A Pedagogy of Hope.* New York: Routledge.
24. 'My silences had not protected me. Your silence will not protect you. But for every real word spoken, for every attempt I had ever made to speak those truths for which I am still seeking, I had made contact with other women while we examined the words to fit a world in which we all believed, bridging our differences': Audre Lorde (2012) *Sister Outsider: Essays and Speeches.* Crossing Press, p. 41.
25. Lorde, A. (1982) *Zami: A New Spelling of My Name.* Massachusetts: Persephone Press; Lorde, *Sister Outsider: Essays and Speeches.*
26. Mirza, H. (1997) *Black British Feminism: A Reader.* London: Routledge.
27. Frankenberg, R. (1993) *White Women, Race Matters. The Social Construction of Whiteness.* Minneapolis: University of Minnesota Press.
28. Lorde, *Zami: A New Spelling of My Name.*
29. Crenshaw, K.W. (1995). 'Mapping the margins: Intersectionality, identity politics, and violence against women of color' in Crenshaw, K., Gotanda, N., Peller, G., and Thomas, K. (eds), *Critical Race Theory: The Key Writings that Formed the Movement.* New York, NY: New Press, pp. 357–83; Taylor, K.-Y. (ed) (2017) *How We Get Free: Black Feminism and the Combahee River Collective.* Chicago: Haymarket; *The Combahee River Collective Statement* (1977) by Combahee River Collective. (https://www.blackpast.org/african-american-history/combahee-river-collective-statement-1977/ [accessed 8 May 2022]).
30. Cited in: Smith, B. (ed.) (1983) *Home Girls: A Black Feminist Anthology.* New York: Kitchen Table: Women of Color Press.
31. See for example: Harding, S. (1997) 'Women's Standpoints on Nature: What Makes Them Possible?', *Women, Gender, and Science: New Directions*, 12: 186–200; Hartsock, N. (1997) 'Comment on Hekman's "Truth and Method: Feminist Standpoint Theory Revisited": Truth or Justice?' *Signs*, 2 (2): 367–74; Smith, B. (ed.) *Home Girl*; Smith, D.E.

(1997) 'Comment on Hekman's "Truth and Method: Feminist Standpoint Theory Revisited"', *Signs* (22)2: 392–8.

32. Lutz, H. (2002) 'Zonder blikken of blozen. Het standpunt van de (nieuw-) realisten', *Tijdschrift voor Genderstudies* 5(3): 7–17.

33. Bunch, C., Myron, N., Brown, R.M., and Berson, G. (1974) *Class and Feminism: A Collection of Essays from the Furies.* Baltimore: Diana Press.

34. Faderman, L. (1991) *Odd Girls and Twilight Lovers: A History of Lesbian Life in Twentieth-Century America.* New York: Columbia University Press; Brown, R.M. (1974) 'The Last Straw' in Bunch et al., *Class and Feminism.*

35. Feinberg commented on *Stone Butch Blues* in her author's note to the 2003 edition: 'Like my own life, this novel defies easy classification. If you found *Stone Butch Blues* in a bookstore or library, what category was it in? Lesbian fiction? Gender studies? Like the germinal novel *The Well of Loneliness by Radclyffe/John Hall,* this book is a lesbian novel and a transgender novel—making 'trans' genre a verb, as well as an adjective …'. See https://www.lesliefeinberg.net/ [accessed 21 December 2020].

36. Duberman, M. (1999) *Left Out: The Politics of Exclusion – Essays 1964– 1999.* New York: Basic Books; Kennedy, E.L. and Davis, M.C. (1993) *Boots of Leather, Slippers of Gold. The History of a Lesbian Community.* New York: Routledge.

37. Nestle, J. (1987) *A Restricted Country.* Michigan: Firebrand Books.

38. Kay, J. (1998) *Trumpet.* London: Picador.

39. Rich, A. (1980) 'Compulsory Heterosexuality and Lesbian Existence', *Women: Sex and Sexuality,* 5(4): 631–60.

40. See Ahmed's (2017) take on reclaiming Rich's maligned 'lesbian continuum'.

41. Wittig, M. (1992) *The Straight Mind and Other Essays.* Boston: Beacon.

42. Butler, J. (1990) *Gender Trouble: Feminism and the Subversion of Identity.* New York: Routledge; Butler, J. (1993) *Bodies That Matter: On the Discursive Limits of Sex.* New York: Routledge; Butler, J. (1993) 'Imitation and Gender Insubordination' in Abelove, H., Barale, A.M,. and Halperin, M.D. (eds), *The Lesbian and Gay Studies Reader.* New York: Routledge, pp. 307–20.

43. Butler *Gender Trouble,* p. 143.

44. Butler, J. (1997) 'Merely Cultural', *Social Text 52/53,*15(3–4): 265–77; Fraser, N. (1997) 'Heterosexism, Misrecognition, and Capitalism: A Response to Judith Butler', *Social Text 52/53,* 15(3–4): 279–89.

45. See for example: Davy, Z (2011). *Recognizing Transsexuals: Personal, Political and Medicolegal Embodiment.* Aldershot: Ashgate Publishing; Pearce, R. (2018) *Understanding Trans Health: Discourse, Power and Possibility.* Bristol: Policy Press; Pearce, R. (2020) 'A Methodology for the Marginalised: Surviving Oppression and Traumatic Fieldwork in the Neoliberal Academy', *Sociology,* 54(4): 806–24; Pearce, R., Moon, I.,

Gupta, K. and Steinberg, D.L. (2019) *The Emergence of Trans Cultures, Politics and Everyday Lives*. London: Routledge; Spade, D. (2011) *Normal Life: Administrative Violence, Critical Trans Politics, and the Limits of Law*. Boston: South End Press; Vincent, B., Erikainen, S., and Pearce, R. (2020) *TERF Wars: Feminism and the Fight for Transgender Futures*. London: Sage.

46. Benavente, G. and Gill-Peterson, J. (2019) 'The Promise of Trans Critique: Susan Stryker's Queer Theory', *GLQ: A Journal of Lesbian and Gay Studies*, 25(1): 23–8.
47. Eng & Puar 'Introduction: Left of Queer'.
48. Cohen, C.J. (1997) 'Punks, Bulldaggers and Welfare Queens. The Radical Potential of Queer Politics', *GLQ: A Journal of Lesbian and Gay Studies*, 3: 437–65.
49. Zabrowskis, M. (2022) 'Exploiting Shared Queer Knowledge' in Mahn, C., Brim, M., and Taylor, Y. (eds) *Queer Sharing in the Marketized University*. London: Routledge.
50. Ahmed, *Living a Feminist Life*.
51. Mackay, F. (2021) *Female Masculinities and the Gender Wars: The Politics of Sex*. London: Bloomsbury.
52. You can read the full speech delivered by Sojourner Truth at the Women's Rights Convention, 1851: https://www.thesojournertruthproject.com/compare-the-speeches/ [accessed 16 February 2022].
53. Muñoz, J.E. (1999) *Disidentifications: Queers of Color and the Performance of Politics*. Minneapolis, MN: University of Minnesota Press.
54. Love, H. (2015) 'Doing Being Deviant: Deviance Studies, Description, and the Queer Ordinary', *Differences. A Journal of Feminist Cultural Studies*, 26(1):74–95.
55. Nash, J. (2019) *Black Feminism Reimagined: After Intersectionality*. Durham, NC: Duke University Press.
56. Olufemi, L. (2020) *Feminism Interrupted: Disrupting Power*. London: Pluto.
57. Organised by Dr Harvey Humphrey and Dr Hazel Marzetti, and funded by the British Sociological Association, as another kind of queer-feminist classroom. See: https://www.eventbrite.co.uk/e/whos-here-whos-queer-making-space-for-queer-ecrs-in-academia-tickets-230379259567# [accessed 16 February 2022], or podcast: https://anchor.fm/strathclyde-education/episodes/Podcast-33-Meet-some-academics-Harvey-Humphrey-and-Yvette-Taylor-e1h6dkg [accessed 14 April 2022].
58. Taylor, Y. (2010) 'The "Outness" of Queer' in Browne, K. and Nash, C. (eds), *Queer Methodologies*. London: Ashgate, pp. 69–84.
59. hooks, b. (1994) *Teaching to Transgress: Education as the Practice of Freedom*. New York: Routledge. See here for an obituary for bell hooks:

https://www.theguardian.com/world/2021/dec/17/bell-hooks-obituary [accessed 17 December 2021].

60. Hennessy, R. (2000) *Profit and Pleasure: Sexual Identities in Late Capitalism.* New York: Routledge.

61. Duggan, L. and Richard K. (2012), 'Preface: A New Queer Agenda', *S&F Online* 10(1–2) (http://sfonline.barnard.edu/a-new-queer-agenda/preface/ [accessed 1 May 2018]).

62. DeFilippis, J. (2012) 'Common Ground: The Queerness of Welfare Policy', *S&F Online* 10(1–2) (https://sfonline.barnard.edu/common-ground-the-queerness-of-welfare-policy/ [accessed 1 May 2018].)

63. Cohen, 'Punks, Bulldaggers and Welfare Queens. The radical potential of queer politics', at; 462.

64. Ferguson, R. (2004) *Aberrations in Black: Toward a Queer of Color Critique.* Minneapolis: University of Minnesota Press.

65. Brim, M. (2020) *Poor Queer Studies*; Mahn et al., *Queer Sharing in the Marketized University*; Taylor, Y., Brim, M., and Mahn, C. (2022) *Queer Precarities In and Out of Higher Education.* London: Bloomsbury.

66. Eng & Puar, K.J. 'Introduction: Left of Queer'.

67. See for example: Ahmed, S. (2010) *On Being Included: Racism and Diversity in Institutional Life.* Durham, NC: Duke University Press; Breeze, M. and Taylor, Y. (2020) *Feminist Repetitions in Higher Education.*

68. Brim, *Poor Queer Studies*, p. 11.

69. Traies, J. (ed) (2021) *Free to Be Me: Refugee Stories from the Lesbian Immigration Support Group.* UK: Tollington Press; Percy, E. (2021) *Duck Feet.* Edinburgh: Monstrous Regiment Publishing Ltd.

70. Berlant, L. and Warner, M. (1995) 'Guest Column: What does Queer Theory Teach us about X?', *Publications of the Modern Language Association of America*, 1: 343–9.

Index

ill refers to an illustration; *n* to a note

7/7 (7th July 2005) 12, 116
9/11 (11th September 2001) 12, 107,
    112, 116, 117, 121

Ahmed, Sara 142
Allison, Dorothy 137
Anzaldúa, Gloria 77, 112, 133
Arani, Alexia 56–7
archives viii, 2, 21–2, 35, 139
Asian women 118–22
asylum seekers 74–5
austerity 13, 83–90, 92, 106–7

Bannon, Ann *Odd Girl Out* 137
bedroom tax 83–4
Berlant, Lauren 18
Berlant, Lauren and Michael Warner
    157
Bishopsgate Institute archive 139
Boyd, Cat 78
Brexit 3, 15–16, 27, 39, 62–73, 77, 81–2
Bridgeton, Glasgow 36
Brim, Matt 153
    Poor Queer Studies 35, 38
British colonialism 26, 71, 77
Butler, Judith *Gender Trouble* 140–1

Cameron, David 88
Census (2011) 26, 67
Census (2021–22) 66
Church of Scotland 100
CILIA project 65–8, 172–3*n*6
citizenship 27, 63, 65, 67
    entitlements of 13, 15, 61, 65, 72,
        82, 85
    impact of Brexit on 61–7

Civil Partnership Act (2004) 94
class 4–5, 9, 10–11, 153
    see also middle class; working class
Coalition Government 2, 13
code-switching 7, 116, 164*n*7
Cohen, Cathy 141–2
    *Punks, Bulldaggers and Welfare
        Queens* 147
Combahee River Collective 111, 148
coming out 114, 130–1
Conservative government 12, 13, 28
conversion therapy 177*n*19
*Covid-19 and the Human Rights of
    LGBT People* (UN Report) 50
Covid-19 pandemic 16, 42–61, 153,
    170*n*13
Creating Feminist Classrooms 152*ill*
Crenshaw, Kimberlé 138, 148
Crisp, Catherine 114–5

DeFilippis, Jacob 147
Disability Living Allowance (DLA) 13,
    83, 90
disabled people 90–1, 101–4
Drumchapel, Glasgow 25, 29, 100,
    166–7*n*6
Duggan, Lisa and Richard Kim *A New
    Queer Agenda* 147
Duggan, Mark 88
Dunn, Etta 168*n*20
Dunne, Gill *Lesbian Lifestyles* 110
Dykes Go Marching On, The! 131, 135

Early-Career Researchers' Workshop
    155
Eng David L. and Jasbir Puar 141

Equality Act (2012) 14, 53, 87, 89, 90,
  95–6, 99, 150
Equality, Diversity and Inclusion
  (EDI) 67–8
European Union (EU) 70–1
  see also Brexit

Federici, Silvia 130–1
feminism 8, 114, 136, 143, 145–6
  see also queer feminism
Frankenberg, Ruth White Women,
  Race Matters 138
Fraser, Nancy 141
Free Church of Scotland 74

gay parents 13–14, 94
gender 140–1
Gender Recognition Act (2004) 53,
  125, 164n4, 171n16
Gender Studies 136–43
Gill-Peterson, Jules 113, 141
  Legacy 163n2
Glasgow 7, 25–6, 29, 121
  'weegie' nickname 26–7, 167n9
Glasgow Women's Library archive
  (GWL) 5–6, 33ill, 34–41, 37ill
Global Financial Crisis (2008) 83

Hall-Carpenter Archive 139
Hennessy, Rosemary 147
homonationalism 63, 70–1, 122

intersectionality 22, 88, 106, 138–9,
  142–3, 149, 151

Johnson, Boris 44, 82, 88

Kafe Kweer, Edinburgh 171n22
Kay, Jackie Trumpet 139
Keating, Shannon 113

Lesbian and Gay Parenting project
  13–14

Lesbian Gay and Bisexual Alliance
  180n20
lesbians 8, 108–16
lesbians of colour 111–2, 148–9
LGTB Action Plan (2018) 3
LGBT Politics Crash Course 89
LGTB+ people 12–13, 44, 163n2
  ethnic groups 66–8
  reading lists for 131–3, 137–40,
    157–8, 158ill, 160–2
  self-identification of 22, 24–5, 68–9
  for topics related to LGTB+ people,
    see the topic, e.g. austerity
Liberal Democrats Party 13
Lorber, Judith 134
Lorde, Audre 148
  Zami: A New Spelling of My Name
    137–8

Making Space for Queer-Identifying
  Religious Youth project 14, 23ill,
    99
Marriage (Same Sex Couples) Act
  (2013) 79, 94, 176–7n15
Metropolitan Community Church
  (MCC) 14–15, 99, 100–1, 106,
    177n22
McIntosh, Peggy 114
middle class queers 8, 69–70, 84, 95–8
mixed race people 124–5
Morocco 74, 76
Morrison, Jenny 78
multiculturalism 11–12
Muñoz, José Esteban 142
Muslim women 40
Muslims 118–9
mutual aid 56–7

Nash, Jennifer 142–3
National Health Service (NHS) 47,
  49–51, 87, 89
  and Covid-19 pandemic 44, 45,
    54–5, 62
New Labour 11–13, 127

Not in Education, Employment or Training (NEET) 101

outreach work 86
Outwrite (newspaper) 129*ill*

parents and parenting 96
see also gay parents
Percy, Ely *Duck Feet* 156
Personal Independence Payments (PIP) 13, 83
Pink Paper 86
Pink Peacock cafe, Glasgow 171–2*n*22
Poverty and Social Exclusion of Lesbians and Gay Men in Glasgow (GWL) 35
precarity 10, 84–5, 130
Pride festival 58
Puar, Jasbir J. 71, 141
Puwar, Nirmal 12

Queer As Folk (tv programme) 11, 165*n*16
queer feminism 106–7, 152–3
queer theory 111, 142, 145–7, 157
Queer/Class Workshop 34–7, 34*ill*, 36*ill*, 38–9, 39*ill*, 40*ill*

race and racism 40, 45, 48, 66–9, 81–2, 112, 114–7, 124
Race Equality Framework for Scotland (2016–30) 167*n*11
Radical Independence Campaign 78
Raffo, Susan 142, 158
Queerly Classed 128
Rainbow Europe 8, 15–16, 63–5, 70–1, 73, 75, 82, 112
rainbow flag 49, 54, 60
Rajan-Rankin, Sweta 77
Rebel Dykes (film) 112–3, 127, 179*n*15
religion 14–15, 99–105, 177*n*19
religious schools 178*n*25
Rich, Adrienne 139–40
Roy, Arundhati 60
Rural Lesbian Group 123

Same Sex Marriage Act *see* Marriage (Same Sex Couples) Act
Scotland 3–4, 74–81
ethnic mix in 26–7, 67
referendum on independence (2014) 3, 15, 78, 89
Scottish Index of Multiple Deprivation (SIMD) 166–7*n*6
Section 28 legislation 12–13, 28
single mothers 95
Skeggs, Bev *Formations of Class and Gender* 32, 137
Souter, Brian 12–13
stigma and stigmatisng 13, 50, 84, 85, 121
Sure Start programme 14

Taylor Yvette
Lesbian and Gay Parenting 13
Working Class Lesbian Life 12–13, 35, 87, 109–10
Tea, Michelle 137
Thatcher, Margaret 28–9
Tipton, Billy 139
Tottenham riots (2011) 88
trans-exclusionary radical feminism (TERF) 8, 113, 142
Truth, Sojourner 142
tuition fees 13, 30
Twitter 145, 151
Tyler, Imogen 93

UK Research and Innovation (UKRI) 166*n*2
University College Union (UCU) strike 128, 130, 130*ill*
university education 29–34

Weeks, Jeffrey [et al.] *Same Sex Intimacies* 110
Welfare Reform Act (2012) 13, 83
Who's Here? Who's Queer Workshop (2022) 144–5, 154*ill*
Wikipedia 25
Wittig, Monique 140

Wollstonecraft, Mary *A Vindication of the Rights of Women* 136
women's libraries 168*n*
working class
  negative stereotyping of 84
  and race 45

working class lesbians 115, 126–7
working class parents 29–30, 98–9
working class queers 8–9, 11, 16–19, 85

young LGBT+ people 14–15, 170*n*14

Thanks to our Patreon subscriber:

Ciaran Kane

Who has shown generosity and
comradeship in support of our publishing.

Check out the other perks you get by subscribing
to our Patreon – visit patreon.com/plutopress.
Subscriptions start from £3 a month.